PENGUIN BOOKS

INDIAN THOUGHT: A MISCELLANY

R.K. Narayan's first novel, *Swami and Friends*, appeared in 1938. Since then he has published fourteen novels, several collections of novellas and short stories as well as essays, travel books and retellings of Indian epics and myths. Undoubtedly the best-known Indian novelist writing in English, he has been translated into many languages, ranging from Hebrew to Japanese. He has received many honours, including the A.C. Benson medal of the Royal Society of Literature. The American Academy of Arts and Letters made him an honorary member, one of the only two Indians to be so honoured. His highly popular novel, *The Guide*, won for him a Sahitya Akademi award and was made into a movie as were several of his short stories. He also served a term as a member of the Rajya Sabha of the Indian Parliament.

Narayan, who turned ninety last year, has also written an autobiography, *My Days*. Penguin Books India has published a number of his books, including *Malgudi Landscapes*, a representative anthology of all aspects of his writing. He lives in Madras.

* * *

S. Krishnan taught English literature at Madras College and at Annamalai University. He la[...] many years with the United States Informatio[...] as a cultural and educational adviser. A freelan[...] and editor, Krishnan is a Consultant Editor [...] *Indian Review of Books*, and a Senior Editor of [...] music and dance magazine. He has edited *M*[...] *Landscapes*, an anthology of R.K. Narayan's w[...] and has translated a Tamil novel, *Tale of A Ta*[...] *Tree*, both published by Penguin Books India.

S. Krishnan lives in Madras.

Indian Thought
A Miscellany

Edited by
R.K. Narayan

With an introduction by
S. Krishnan

PENGUIN BOOKS

Penguin Books India (P) Ltd., 11 Community Centre, Panchsheel Park, New
Delhi 110017, India
Penguin Books Ltd., 80 Strand, London WC2R 0RL, UK
Penguin Putnam Inc., 375 Hudson Street, New York, NY 10014, USA
Penguin Books Australia Ltd., Ringwood, Victoria, Australia
Penguin Books Canada Ltd., 10 Alcorn Avenue, Suite 300, Toronto,
Ontario M4V 3B2, Canada
Penguin Books (NZ) Ltd., Cnr Rosedale and Airborne Roads, Albany, Auckland,
New Zealand

First published by Penguin Books India 1997

Copyright © R. K. Narayan 1997

Typeset in *New Brunswick* by SURYA, New Delhi-110 011

Printed at Basu Mudran, Kolkata

Contents

Introduction

'*Indian Thought* overwhelmed and frightened me—it had an orange wrapper with my name on it, with a spreading banyan tree and a full moon behind silhouetting a tramp lounging in its shade,' recalls Narayan in his autobiography, *My Days*. Orange wrapper? The only copies— probably the only ones in existence—of the three issues that the writer has seen have grey covers. Unless Narayan meant that each copy came wrapped in orange-coloured paper. The letterpress on the cover stated: *Indian Thought, a Quarterly journal, edited by R.K. Narayan ... Volume 1 1941 No. 1 . . . April-May-June*. The list of contents was displayed in full—a practice that Narayan gave up with the subsequent issues. Three issues appeared in that year, at more or less quarterly intervals. A fourth issue was edited, typeset and perhaps even printed, but it never saw the light of day. In the manner of little magazines the world over, *Indian Thought* too sank without a trace, aided and abetted by the printer, and mourned not even by its editor. The only people who may have shed a tear over it were perhaps some of the contributors who were fondly hoping to see themselves in print in the next issue. The truth was that it simply became impossible to run the magazine in the middle of all the hassles that war-time conditions created, such as obtaining the necessary paper. Editing and publishing *Indian Thought* acted as the final spur to free Narayan from the melancholy that had shrouded him like a black cloud since the death of his beloved wife, and put him back on the path of his vocation: writing. The dabbling in journalism led him so surely back to writing that two years later he produced *The English Teacher*, the finest of his novels, and a watershed in his creative endeavour. From here on he would be more the amused spectator than the involved participant in his fiction.

Rasipuram Krishnaswamy Ayyar Narayanaswamy (mercifully, he shortened the name to its present form, partly at the instance of his good friend, Graham Greene, when he published his first novel, *Swami and Friends*) was born in Madras on 10 October 1906 in his grandmother's house. His father was a headmaster in the Mysore State school system, who was transferred frequently from one school to another. By the time he arrived on the scene, Narayan had already a brood of siblings, so his grandmother decided to keep him in Madras to provide some relief to his overworked mother. Here he grew up in a rambling house with a peacock and a monkey for company. Lovingly supervised by his grandmother and an uncle, he went to neighbourhood schools, until his final school year when he was recalled to Mysore, where his father had become the headmaster of the prestigious Maharaja's Collegiate High School, which had a university entrance class. Not that it did Narayan any good. 'Next to religion, education was the most compulsive force at home in a family like ours. My outlook on education never fitted in the accepted code at home. I instinctively rejected both education and examination, with their unwarranted seriousness and esoteric suggestions.' Despite his father being something of a martinet both as headmaster and as parent, Narayan managed to fail for two successive years in the university entrance examination—a blessing in disguise as it turned out to be. Mysore in those days (and even now to a certain extent) was a cool city with charming vistas, tree-lined roads, a low hill straight out of a fairy tale, tanks and lakes, and Narayan went on endless walks, always carrying with him a book from the school library. He read widely and eclectically, and he also began writing, with his younger brothers and their friends jollying him along in his endeavours. Eventually, he took a BA degree. His first totally unwilling efforts to earn a living as a teacher proved disastrous. So he stayed home, reading and writing, earning a few rupees by contributing reports to a magazine in Madras—no great burden on his joint family. He also started writing *Swami and Friends* which was published in London in 1937. The charming and dusty little town of Malgudi, with its winding lanes and eccentric inhabitants was born. Graham Greene helped find a publisher for the book as well as for the two that followed, *The Bachelor of Arts* and *The Dark Room*. They achieved a considerable *succes d' estime* from reviewers but sold negligibly. The unsold copies were destroyed by a blitzkrieg during the Second World War.

In the meantime, Narayan fell in love with a girl he had watched drawing water from a street tap. The course of true love certainly did not run smooth in this case—the ultimate *sine qua non* of a Hindu marriage—the horoscopes of the boy and girl, did not match. However, after a lot of resistance, Narayan married Rajam, but astrology would seem to have had the last word. After five blissful years, during the course of which the couple had a baby daugher, Rajam died of typhoid in 1939. To say that Narayan was disconsolate would be a ridiculous understatement. He retired into himself altogether, with only the child providing his sole link with everyday life. He went to Madras for a change with the little girl, and here, the psychic experiences he had with a couple who conducted seances and recorded messages from departed souls on paper, reconciled him to his loss. He returned to Mysore, an almost serene man, ready to go on with the business of living. Though convinced that he would never write a book again, he started contributing desultory pieces to Madras magazines. The year 1941 thus found him entrenched in his large joint family, delighting in his four-year-old daughter, and spending some time with old friends in the evenings in the clinic of a doctor which served as a meeting place, until supplanted by the Boardless, a restaurant unique in that it had no signboard. Here, one day, the idea of *Indian Thought* was mooted.

One of the advantages of being the headmaster's son was infinite access to the school library. As we have already seen, Narayan drew from it books ranging from Scott to Mrs Henry Wood to suit his disorganized reading. But a further advantage was that the magazines that the school subscribed to were delivered at the headmaster's house just before the weekend. Narayan's father did not mind his and his brother reading them first as long as they were returned unspoilt on Monday morning. Also, by using unspent funds from other departments of the school for ordering magazines, the headmaster obtained for his school a fine collection of the latest British and American journals. As a consequence, the boys' weekend reading was 'full and varied'. In his autobiography, Narayan lists some of the magazines he read avidly. They ranged from *Boy's Own Paper* to *Nineteenth Century and After*. From the *Strand*, one of the most popular magazines of Britain which died a natural death when the Second World War ended, he developed a passion for Conan Doyle and P.G. Wodehouse—masters of narrative who surely left their mark on his own writing. He learnt about what such literary figures as Bernard Shaw, H.G. Wells and Thomas Hardy were doing from the *Bookman*, which gave glimpses of their latest works. 'I knew precisely what they said or thought of each other, how much they earned in royalties, and what they were working on at any given moment . . . the scintillating literary world of London was absorbing to watch. From our room, leaning on our pillows in obscure Bojanna Lines of Mysore, we watched the literary personalities strutting about in London.' Add to these the London *Mercury, John o' London, T.P.'s Weekly*, as well as *The Spectator, The Time Literary Supplement* and the *Guardian*, and one can understand what a comprehensive knowledge Narayan had about the periodical literature of the time. *Harper's*, the *Atlantic* and the *American Mercury* kept him informed about what was happening in the fields of art, culture and literature on the other side of the Atlantic Ocean. 'Slowly, I became familiar with critics who mattered and their judgement. Gradually I began . . . also to acquire through the book reviews a critical sense.'

In India too, there was a regular flurry of activity in the field of periodical journalism. The journals that were devoted to specialized subjects had their own audience, but popular journals in English did not do too well. There were fly-by-night magazines, vaguely salacious and scabrous, which died an early death, and political magazines—actually they were no more than pamphlets—which made brief manic appearances before fading away. There were also one or two really popular magazines, with insouciant names like *Merry Magazine*, whose sole purpose was to entertain. This they did quite well, by stealing from writers like P.G. Wodehouse, though they generously gave space to local talent—Narayan published a short story in *Merry Magazine*. But the *My Magazines* and *Merry Magazines* vanished by the time the second half of the century began. The renewed accessibility of foreign magazines after the War may have had something to do with this and in any event, a new culture was slowly but surely replacing the old.

Two Indian magazines, though, held their

ground for a long time, simply because of their excellence, and their nationalist goals, both clearly aligning themselves with the Indian Independence movement. *Modern Review* and *Indian Review* were required reading for the intellectual. *Indian Review* was the precursor. It was started in 1900 by G.A. Natesan, a prominent member of the intellectual and political elite of Madras, who was a close friend of many of the political leaders of the time, and who was host to Mahatma Gandhi during some of the visits of the latter to Madras. The magazine was intended to devote itself to Indian culture in all its manifold aspects, but found itself surely and constantly veering towards politics. Natesan also had a publishing company, which produced inexpensive books about the nationalist movement and its leaders, as well as about spiritual leaders and publicists. The magazine published a book review and a short story by Narayan. *Modern Review*, edited and published by Ramanand Chatterjee from Calcutta, began publication in 1907, and soon established itself as a pre-eminent periodical. Though its coverage was primarily literary and cultural, it covered political and economic topics as well, providing outstanding in-depth articles by leading intellectuals.

So, when Narayan decided to plunge into periodical journalism, he had an ample background. In addition to his deep knowledge of what it required to produce a journal, he had had successful forays in the field as a contributor. He had written for *The Hindu* for some years more or less on a regular basis, and he had even had a satirical piece published in *Punch*, an accomplishment in those days next only to getting the Nobel Prize. When it was suggested that he should start a publication of his own, he was ready. 'During one of these sessions (at the clinic), I cannot say whose idea it was, but the idea was born that I should start a publication of my own. I rejected the proposal for obvious reasons,' says Narayan in his autobiography, but that last statement is something of a *non sequitur*. For he goes on to add: 'Purna (his friend who had Graham Greene interested in his first book), who used to float in and out of this group constantly, suggested puckishly, "Why not call it *Indian Thoughtless*?" "Let us call it *Indian Thought*, which will amount to the same thing," said another.' We see that Narayan seamlessly moved from non-acceptance to acquiescence. The group then worked out the details, decided it would be 'a quarterly publication, devoted to literature, philosophy and culture'. Perhaps, subconsciously it was the stimulus that he was waiting for. He goes on to add: 'I could hardly sleep that night. My head buzzed with plans and calculations.' He spent the next days preparing an editorial manifesto, no more pompous than others of its kind. 'I packed into the manifesto all my ambition: to phrase our culture properly: to utilize English as a medium for presenting our cultural heritage . . .' Despite all his later misgivings, he did succeed to a certain extent in achieving his goal.

He got going with the manic earnestness of one of his own characters, wrote letters to all and sundry drawing their attention to the magazine-to-be, inviting contributions from others, and looking around for somebody to print and produce the magazine. He ran into the right person almost immediately: Cheluviengar, a stage-struck printer who was the proprietor of the City Power Press, and whose whole being was dedicated to acting in and producing stage plays. (Later, he was to become a character-actor in over a hundred Kannada movies.) Narayan's good fortune in finding Cheluviengar as his printer was two-fold—the man turned out to be an enthusiastic partner in the project, and he also became a leading character in one of Narayan's finest novels, *Mr Sampath* (Cheluviengar was universally known as Sampath.) Amiable and friendly, and with no real thought for money, Sampath owned a treadle machine, and his promises had nothing to do with one's expectations. His good humour always warded off any annoyance on the part of a client whose work had taken much longer than promised. It took three months for Sampath to produce the first issue of *Indian Thought*. 'After I had given up in despair', Sampath knocked on my door one midnight, and there he stood on the verandah holding out to me dramatically the first copy of *Indian Thought* and a thousand more waiting to be unloaded from a tonga at the gate. He looked triumphant as he said, ". . . if matter for the next issue is ready, I'd like to start it right away—my machines cannot remain idle, they are now geared for your job—you have no idea how many jobs I have had to turn down." '

The ethical aspects of producing the magazine were more problematic for Narayan than fighting a losing battle with Sampath's treadle. He was being constantly given articles which no one in his right mind would want to read. A story he published turned out to be plagiarized from Wodehouse. His landlord, who wanted to evict the family from his house, attempted blackmail—if Narayan would publish one of his contributions, he would hold off the eviction. Narayan allowed himself to be blackmailed, but did not like himself one bit for doing so. 'When I read the story in cold print in the third number, I felt ashamed of myself as an editor: I felt I had prostituted my position for a domestic cause, and that my readers would be justified in stoning me at sight.'

The production of the magazine finally became a nightmare. Sampath's amiability was really no substitute, for, his non—or rather—delayed-performance was taking a toll on Narayan's nerves. The struggle for obtaining paper for the magazine was becoming worse by the day. 'It had all become so nerve-wracking that I decided to put an end to the publication with the fourth number.' Ironically, the magazine was a financial success at the time of its demise—with the help of his uncle in Madras the paid subscription of the magazine had gone beyond a thousand—a no mean number then or now. In retrospect, it was fun while it lasted.

Looking at it more than fifty years after it was published, one finds unexpected delights in *Indian Thought*. It deals with a world which many of us have no conception of. There is a spaciousness to personality which today is constricted into mean, little egos. The language of the pieces is often pure to the point of sounding archaic. There was a war going on in the outside world, but it hardly casts a shadow on the writing or content. It is worth taking a look at some of the contributors who give the magazine its unique flavour.

Narayan was bitterly experienced in the matter of rejection slips. Almost everything he sent to an editor in the early days, usually in London, came back to him with a rejection slip, kindly, casual or neutral in tone. So when he started his own journal, he remembered the rejection slips 'and decided I would not be like them. I was destined to discover and nurture a whole school of young writers. If I were to reject an article, I'd write a letter more in sorrow than in arrogance, and never send a printed rejection slip under any circumstances.' At this distance, one suspects that Narayan did not really have to meet this dilemma, for almost all the writers in *Indian Thought* are fairly well-known figures.

The first piece in the first issue is a short story by C. Rajagopalachari, one of the leading national figures of the country who had, at that time of writing, already been the chief minister of Madras Presidency, and was later to become the last Governor-General of India. He was erudite and scholarly, and was given to writing stories which usually had an ambiguous ending. Narayan had one such story translated from Tamil to serve as the showpiece of his first issue. Other prominent personalities, then or now, who contributed to the magazine included Paul Brunton, the mystic, who searched for ancient mysteries that he could unveil in the pyramids of Egypt and elsewhere. He lived in Mysore for a while, and Narayan and he became close friends. The magazine included a typical piece of stream-of-consciousness writing by him, a meditation in mid-Atlantic. Faithful to its original intent, the magazine had translations from classical Sanskrit and Tamil. Two pieces by Dr M.N. Srinivas, the great social anthropologist, are especially noteworthy. One, written as a straightforward story with an O. Henry ending, and the other, a travel write-up about a trip to Mercara in Coorg, already indicate the humanist lines that his research writing would take. Another curious item is the 'letters to a friend'. These were written by Professor Quentin-Anderson to Narayan's father. The good professor did not last long in Mysore because of machinations by several who were hostile to him, but he struck up an enduring friendship with Narayan's father, a friendship which had its ups and downs, as the letters reveal. Narayan admired, and still does, their literary quality.

As is obvious, during the short span of its life, Narayan could not obviously find for the magazine new talent which he could nurture. If he had, he would surely have published some of them. As it is, the magazine is really full of works by friends and relatives. This does not detract in any fashion from the quality of the magazine, since the contributors in most cases were good writers with distinct points of view.

Of course, what is of special interest to us now is Narayan's own contributions to *Indian Thought*. The three issues carry four short stories/ sketches and a playlet under his own name, and a second playlet for which he uses his wife's name as a pseudonym. The plays reveal his interest in making myths relevant, and in depicting loyalty as a virtue in itself. The short stories, some of them published elsewhere, clearly provide enough evidence of the course that his future stories would take—a basic theme, strong construction, characters fully developed, and compassion and empathy.

Reminiscing about his magazine in his autobiography, Narayan expresses considerable dissatisfaction with it. Between the idea and the reality fell a shadow, he seems to be saying. 'I brightened the second number with a deliberate effort—abandoned the orange cover with the silhouette of a tramp, and gave it some less ascetic appearance; included jokes and *obiter dicta* at page-ends as space-fillers. I soon realized that the fillers read better than the stuff occupying the main space on a page. What the journal was in my anticipation was a readable light magazine, every page alive with style and life, profoundity with a light touch. What it actually turned out to be was a hotchpotch of heavy-weight academics and Wodehouse rehash—the sort of journal I would normally avoid.' This is a very harsh self-assessment, and a dismissal of a very important phase in his own development. The magazine has a special importance today as a period piece, reflecting the values of an older time. Those interested in language would revel in the till then unpolluted English in which most of the contributions are written. Produced during the height of the Second World War, the issues provide a serene experience, far removed from the *sturm und drang* going on in the outside world. All in all, *Indian Thought* is a reflection of the personality of its creator—gentle, amused, compassionate, and at the same time, uncomitted and objective.

Once he cast *Indian Thought* aside, Narayan plunged into his serious writing, and *The English Teacher*, wholly autobiographical, came out in 1945, followed by a series of novels and short stories which have earned for him worldwide renown. However, *Indian Thought* did not pass into oblivion. It was built into the name of his publishing house, Indian Thought Publications.

This volume has rearranged the contents of the three issues in discrete sections. The fillers that Narayan mentions with a kind of melancholy distaste have all been left out, as also a couple of items which, neither when published nor now, seem to match the rest of the material.

S. Krishnan

About Indian Thought

We hope to publish (in the course of the year):

* Stories and general literary works translated into English from the various languages in India.

* Serious studies in philosophy, history, art, science, etc.

* Vignettes of Sanskrit literature and philosophy.

* Original literary works in English, and lighter writing.

* Articles on social reconstruction, education etc., which may have a practical value.

This will be the plan of our journal, and we hope it indicates sufficiently our scope and purpose. We prefer to leave it at that since we do not wish to make abstract claims with such expressions as 'Renaissance', 'Culture' and so on.

The word *Indian* in the title is not to be taken to indicate any rigid limitation or reserve either in the choice of subjects or of writers. Nor the word *Thought* to be taken as an unswerving allegiance to metaphysics. We accept the following definition of Thought: 'Thought is man's final reality and embraces *vision* as well as *activity*.'

Short Stories

Rayappan

by
C. Rajagopalachari

Rayappan is one of our paper boys. He is a Christian, but strangely enough, every night he goes to a Vinayaka temple, worships, and sleeps by the side of the idol. Even if you suggested a better place he would not care to go there.

If you asked why he did it, he would just try to laugh it away. If pressed he would say, 'It gives me peace.' 'Was your father a Christian or did you become a Christian yourself?' people sometimes asked. 'I became Christian myself,' he would proudly declare and run off to sell his paper.

* * *

Kandaswami Iyer was the *Karnam* of a village in Krishnagiri. Six months after his child was born his wife slipped and fell into the Devil's

Pond. She went down screaming: 'Alas! What is to happen to my child?' A few years later Kandaswamy Iyer married again. Everything seemed to go on well for a while, but gradually differences arose between the boy Venkataraya and his stepmother. A reasonless dislike grew and ripened. She beat him for being disobedient. He went to his father crying, and he too cursed and beat him. The boy was puzzled. If anyone stoned or beat a street dog and it ran away howling, Venkataraya would say, 'Poor dog! It suffers as I suffer,' and stand watching it for a long time.

Venkataraya was seven years old. He was sent to a school. He had no inclination for studies. His teachers could do nothing with him. They bullied him, and even thrashed him now and then. 'Utter idiot, no use,' they said and left him alone in course of time.

* * *

One day Savarimuthu, a classmate, took Venkataraya to his house. Savarimuthu's mother was at the door eagerly waiting for his return. As soon as he came, she rushed forward, caught him in her arms, and took him in. She asked Savarimuthu: 'Who is this boy?' He replied, 'He is in my class, the son of the *Karnam*. Won't you give him some sweets?' Everything in Savari's house surprised Venkataraya. He could not understand why his own mother was different.

He wished his friend's mother had also been his. A few days later he took Savari aside and asked him: 'How are mothers got? How did you obtain yours?' Savari could not find an answer. He had never thought of the origin of mothers. He said, 'God gives us mothers. For some reason he has not given you a good one. Perhaps he is angry with you.'

Just then Savari's mother came in.

'Mother, this boy's mother is always beating him. Why hasn't he a good mother like you?'

Mary Amma—Savari's mother—smiled at this. She said 'If you are a good boy, your mother won't beat you.' 'When did I get my mother? And when did you come?' he asked Mary Amma. She shook with laughter: 'Poor boy! He doesn't seem to know anything. See here, child! When you were a baby your mother slipped and fell into the Devil's Pond and died. Your father married again. I attended the wedding. The woman who beats you is not your mother. Your mother died long ago.'

Venkataraya opened his eyes wide and asked: 'Where is my mother now?'

'My child, ask God. Your mother will come to you.'

'Who is God? Where can I ask him?'

'My boy, see there! See that picture!' she said pointing at the picture of St Mary hanging aloft the wall.

Venkataraya stood gazing at the picture for

a long time. He felt a strange peace coming over him. On his way home he passed the church. He stopped and peeped in through a window. There too hung a large picture on the wall. He stood gazing at it. Gradually the picture assumed life and, a woman, an embodiment of love, got down from the wall. The next moment she was by his side. A great joy welled up within him as he realized that in answer to his prayer his mother was at his side. 'My child Venkataraya', she said. Ah, her voice! And at the gentle touch of her hands on his face, he was entranced. Venkataraya had attained his mother! She held him in her arms and kissed him. 'Come with me,' she said and took him somewhere. They walked a long way. She stopped now and then to take him in her arms. She said: 'Oh, child! You have been suffering so much these days. Why didn't you call me sooner?'

'I did not know, mother,' Venkataraya said and wept.

'Don't cry,' she said and wiped his eyes with the end of her sari. After walking a long way they were at the house of the Padre. The house was behind a garden. Stopping at the gate Venkataraya said, 'This is a good place. Let us sit in the garden and spend our time. If I go back to my house, she will thrash me.'

He tried to enter the gate.

'Don't go there,' said his mother and tried to stop him.

'Why? What if we go in?' asked Venkataraya.

'Don't. Someone may come. If anyone comes I can't stay, I shall have to go away.'

'I am thirsty. I must drink the water in that well. Come, let us go in,' he said, and dragged her into the gate. 'My child, who are you?' asked the Padre, taking the cigar from his mouth, and coming near him. Mother disappeared.

'Mother, mother!' Venkataraya screamed. 'Where are you gone? Come! Come!' he said and ran hither and thither among the trees. The Padre pacified the boy and took him in, and gave him water. 'Child, who are you?' he asked. The boy had high fever.

* * *

'Child, Jesus alone can save us. He is God's only, and incomparable son. See, there is his picture. His grace will be on you. And then, that is a picture of his Holy Mother. It is she, with love and grace, who brought you here and went away.'

'No, no, It was my mother who brought me here. Not Mary. I will seek her out. I cannot live without seeing her,' cried Venkataraya and ran out with his fever on. It was dark. The Padre allowed him to go and did not follow him.

He roamed hither and thither and reached the temple of Vinayaka. It was deserted, since it was not a Shandy day. A little lamp, lit by someone, was dimly burning before the image.

He threw himself down there. Muttering 'Mother, mother,' he lay for a while and fell asleep. At midnight he sat up suddenly. His mother was beside him. 'Mother' he cried and held her tight. 'You won't leave me again?'

'No, no,' she replied and fondled him. 'Come here and sleep every night. I will also come. I cannot come during the day.' Before dawn she disappeared.

Since then every night Venkataraya slept in the Vinakaya temple. His face acquired a new radiance. All day long he sang and loafed about. The village folk thought him to be mad and pitied him, while Venkataraya splashed and gambolled in a sea of joy. At night he went round Vinakaya thrice and lay down. His mother would come unfailingly. Many days passed thus.

* * *

'How sad, such a young child should have come to this state!' whispered the mothers gathered at the tank.

'Oh, he is only pretending,' said Kandaswami Iyer's wife. 'Pretending or not, God alone knows!' said Kandaswami Iyer to quieten his mind. He felt disgust and anger when he saw the other children of the place.

* * *

One day Venkataraya went to the temple as usual. The Vinakaya was missing. The temple itself had been taken down and lay about as bricks and pillars. Some wealthy man had decided to renovate the temple and earn divine grace. Work had commenced and they had removed the idol temporarily somewhere. Amidst the debris Venkataraya sat all night, sleepless and silent. His mother did not come to him that night. His madness had cleared. The world once again stretched before him parched of love.

He went to the church one day. He peeped in through the old window. He saw on the wall the picture of St Mary. She looked like his mother no doubt, but no one descended from the picture. The picture remained a picture.

✳ ✳ ✳

For a long time he wandered about the debris of the old temple and the church, keenly searching, like one who had lost something. One day he went to the Padre again: 'Sir, let me become a Christian,' he said. The Padre took him in and made very kind enquiries. The following conversation took place between the Padre and Kandaswami Iyer:

'Mr Iyer, through the grace of St Mary your son's madness has left him. He asks to be baptized. Let us not hinder God's will.'

'Alas! We are Brahmins. It is impossible.'

'Let it be. There is no other way. Whether feigned or real, let him be free from his madness, and live somewhere. Please agree to it,' said

Kandaswami Iyer's wife. 'Rama! Rama! Don't say that,' said Kandaswami Iyer. The Padre didn't insist. He dropped the matter.

* * *

And then one day the boy was not to be seen in the village. He disappeared somewhere. He ran away to Madras, and was baptized by a big priest. And Venkataraya became Rayappan. He became a paper-seller. His father and mother know nothing of it. Although a Christian, whenever he sees the stone image of Vinayaka he stops and brings his palms together in salute. And at night he always sleeps beside a Vinayaka. It looks as though he hopes to meet his mother still. The other paper boys are very fond of him.

* * *

'A story need not be very rational; but it must have some significance. It would be nice if you explained a little,' said *Ananda Vikatan*.

'No significance. Just peace of mind. That is all,' said Rajaji with a laugh.

'What, are you trying to laugh it away like Rayappan! Are you preaching against second marriages?'

'No, no. Marriage is always good.'

'Or are you praising the worship of Vinayaka?'

'All right, have it thus. But any worship is good, isn't it?'

'Or are you trying to warn stepmothers?'

'Do stepmothers read your journal? If they do, it will do them good.'

'In these days second wives look after children more devotedly than the mothers themselves,' said *Vikatan*.

'May be,' said Rajaji. 'Times have changed. But you see the duties of a foster-mother in other things. A woman who gets a little girl as her daughter-in-law becomes her foster-mother. A lady engaging a little servant for wages is also a sort of foster-mother. The aristocrat bringing up a little pup is in the relation of a foster-mother to it. Any entity with a growing body and mind and the one who has the responsibility of tending it (man or woman) assume the relationship of child and foster-mother. Mother's is the only natural love in the world. For other kinds of love it is a model. Others must, with care, discrimination, and piety, conduct themselves like mothers. The growing body is to be nourished on ghee; the growing soul has to be nourished on love; without it the soul will be parched.'

'This gives us a headache,' said *Vikatan*. 'Please stop your discourse. As usual you are, we suppose, translating from Sanskrit and talking. Where we are concerned we look after our paper boys as well as we can. A rather mischievous lot, no doubt, but we don't lose our patience.'

'I am glad to hear it. Look after Rayappan

particularly well. If sometimes his behaviour is puzzling, don't get angry with him; send him away to a Vinayaka temple.'

This story is published by kind permission of *Ananda Vikatan* of Madras in which it originally appeared in Tamil.

Garden

by
R.K. Narayan

The Talkative Man said:

At the end of a period of gardening you may have flowers and fruits and vegetables around you, but you will have lost your soul. It is worse than drink and women.

As you see me, I am sure I strike you very favourably, as a fellow full of sense, goodness and sympathy. I am proud to tell you that I come of a family which has possessed these traits for ten generations now. And yet there was a time, a dark period of my life, when I hugged the devil. Now I can see how people must have quailed at the sight of me and prayed for some blight to carry me off. Happily, all that is old story.

I was working for Soil Foods Ltd., Manufacturers of Chemical Fertilizers. I was expected to persuade our peasants to use chemical fertilizers for their crops in place of cowdung and other odds and ends. My area was Malgudi District.

Living is cheap in Malgudi; and for twenty rupees I secured a neat bungalow with a good compound (ah, that was my ruin) on the very edge of the town. I engaged a cook and a servant and I was on the whole very happy and contented.

For amiability, good fellowship, and generosity, my name had become a byword in the town. My gate was always open and vagrants and beggars, visitors and cows, freely came in, went about and did what they liked. Some slept in the shady corners of the compound; some even came up to the veranda; and some unknown persons even lived in the shed. The sight of them always made me happy, and if I did not share my food with them it was because I could not afford it.

My work was light, and in course of time I turned to gardening. One morning I sliced out my compound into several beds and plots; and shooed off all my unknown friends. I told them if they showed themselves again, I would call in the police.

A person like me who loved all animate and inanimate things suddenly realized that the scheme of the universe was opposed to all my most cherished plans. When I sowed the tiny seeds of brinjals and saw next morning that about twenty thousand small ants had opened a camp on the plot, I paused, and frowned to reflect—probably my first frown in life. I removed the camp as gently as I could to another place. But the next morning they were back there, and for yards around every ant in the area carried a tiny seed in its mouth. At the sight of this I felt something slipping within me. I went in. Water was boiling in a kettle. I brought the kettle down and poured the water on the ant camp, and felt relieved at the sight of their small red bodies bleaching and curling up. Thereafter I slaughtered ants wherever I saw them. Remember, I would not hurt any living creature till then.

Next I turned my attention to sparrows. These feathered friends of man subsist on germinating seeds. They usually wait in flocks near every garden plot, watch for soft white sprouts to show themselves above the earth, and then nip them off with their tiny beaks. The few seeds that I saved from the ants ended their career in the gizzards of these birds. I had a gun licence. One day I sat up with the gun in the veranda, opened fire, and mounted a few trophies on bamboo poles as a warning to all sparrow-kind.

I told you I had a servant. He had a son about seven years old. He was an attractive youngster with a perfectly flat nose and the complexion of ebony; and the dirt of a dustbin was on him. He was my best friend in the locality. The fellow owned a small iron hoop and he spent his waking hours pushing it about. In the beginning he was content to roll it about in the backyard. But I encouraged him to come and play in the front compound.

And there I had now planted some jasmine cuttings, roses, and some gorgeous annuals. I suddenly realized that the youngster was a danger to civilization. The change of the place from a wilderness to a well-ordered garden did not at all strike him as a matter worth a man's notice. He went about pushing his hoop as before. I warned him to keep off the front compound and to confine his activities to an uncultivated corner of the backyard. The next day I saw marks of tiny feet on the bed of annuals, and I hunted him down and shouted at him. On the third day I discovered that the fellow would not miss for anything the thrill of running precariously on the edge of cultivated plots. And so when the boy was away, I gathered some thorns and strewed them on the edge of the flower beds. I sat in the veranda and watched, and when the boy came and collapsed with a howl on the geranium plot, leaving his hoop to roll away, I felt triumphant. I went over to him and gently kicked him. The boy stood gazing at me, quite baffled by my new manner. I dragged him by the ear to the gate and pushed him out, and threw his iron hoop after him. The hoop must have hit him somewhere, because his father came to me and said that some beast had hurt his son with iron. I told the man that I would crack his son's skull if he came near my garden again. He had been an ideal servant with the courtesy of a prince and the efficiency of a machine, but he loved his son dearly; and he replied that he would see my head broken first. I dismissed him on the spot. He spread the rumour that I drank heavily; and I could not get another servant at any price. After this I did not live, as you will presently see, very long in Malgudi; but the few months I stayed there, I cleaned my shoes, swept my house, and in various other ways acquired self-reliance.

Mark my progress. I have told you that in the pre-gardening days my gates were always open. In those days, at a time, about twenty-four cows could be seen in my compound, grazing on the God-given grass. I loved to see in the languid afternoons, white cows munching grass, and the cow-boys dozing under the margosa tree. It was a picture that produced in me a certain spiritual satisfaction. After I became a gardener, naturally I had to forego this pleasure. But it hit the cows as well as their owners hard.

I need hardly tell you that milkmen in our country own cows but not food or shelter for them. In the off-hours the animals are turned out to shift for themselves. They lounge in the marketplace, promenade the busy thoroughfares, and try the gate of every bungalow in the town and live mostly on gardens.

Now everyday I had to carry out a big cattle drive in my place. There were gaps in the lantana fencing and my gate was weak, and cows invaded my compound. I chased them about and many a cow of the place bore the mark of my stick on its back. Remember, I am a Hindu, and the cow is very sacred to me! I strengthened the fencing and secured the gate with heavy bolts. This kept the cows out during the day; but early in the morning, I saw hoof marks in my garden, and plants that had stood yards high on the previous evening would now be mere stumps at ground level. I sat up one night in the dark veranda and watched. The milk-men came at dead of night, jumped over the gate, drew the bolt back, let the cows in, shut the gate again, and went away. Early in the morning, at milking time, they took the cows out and closed the gate before going. This arrangement was evidently considered satisfactory to both parties. I should have the satisfaction of not seeing the cows and they of not letting their cows starve. When I caught them, I meted out punishment in several ways: sent the cows to the Municipal pound, kicked the cow-owners when they came to beg that it should not be done, and lodged a police complaint, so that they were kicked by the police too.

Lastly, through a gap in the fencing, my compound served as a short-cut between a nearby village and the local law courts. A foot-track ran through the compound and it was much in use. I had first permitted custom to have its way because the sight of people passing from village to court made me happy.

Now I put up boards on all sides warning trepassers and closed the gap in the fencing. But the percentage of literacy in our country is low and it does not take much time to make gaps in fences. The trespassers gathered the harvests of my garden and walked on the seedlings. For a week I kept shouting at them, and then lost my head one day and ran after two village litigants. I went for them with such a war-whoop that they started running. I chased them down the road and kicked and rolled them down in the dust.

The litigants staggered to the courts with contusions and bruises. Their lawyers suggested a suit for assault as a profitable line of action. The owners of cows had also got in touch with the lawyers and further suits for assault were hatched.

There were one or two police cases against me for assault and about three suits for damages. They took all my time and most of my savings.

These cases brought me such a notoriety that every man, woman and child in the town shuddered at the sight of me. The town had never known such a drunkard and bully . . .

This reputation naturally affected my business. My average daily sales till now had been about four hundred pounds of chemical fertilizers, but now it had gradually shrunk to about fifty.

The plot I cherished most was one containing about ten Shoe-Flower plants. They were a special variety—the purple kind with a double row of petals. I had secured them with great difficulty from one of my customers, and they were coming up quite well, but somehow I felt that they were not growing fast enough. Caught by a sudden experimental mood, one day, I mixed in their soil an ounce of 'Palitate', a special preparation of our company's for gardens. And four days later there were only ten charred stumps in that plot.

I believe I cried a little. I squatted under a tree and sat brooding. The postman came and gave me a letter. It was from my office containing scathing references to my recent work and demanding an explanation. This was not an auspicious moment for my office to send me that letter. I went in and wrote a reply informing my employers that there was a limit to the gullibility of the public, that it would not go on giving money in exchange for blights like 'Palitate'; and that the company had better change its name from Soil Foods to Soil Poisons Ltd.

Next day I received a wire summoning me to

the head office. I knew the end had come.

I sat under a tree and held a review of my activities. I saw where I was (and why) very clearly.

I looked about the garden. I had created a feast for the eye, nose, and the tongue. The plants ached with their load of flowers and fruits . . .

I took a stout stick and laid it about me. In about half an hour there was not one plant standing vertically in the compound. I went to the gate and threw it wide open. There were half a dozen cows waiting outside. I invited them in. They had apparently been starving for a long time.

I lost my job. I secured another only after two years of intense travail—that is another story. I shall close this with a moral: if you see only dry grass in your compound, leave it alone; never try to grow brinjals or roses in its place.

A Parrot Story

by
R.K. Narayan

Ramani resolved to become a parrot-trader when
he saw the following advertisement in a local
newspaper:

> 'Wanted a parrot trained to repeat the holy
> names of gods and *slokas*. Preferably in a
> musical manner. Prepared to pay Rs 10/-
> to Rs 100/- according to the qualification
> of the parrot. Communications to be
> addressed to . . .'

This advertisement caught his eye at a time
when he was keenly searching for a congenial
occupation. He was a poet, author of *Blood-
Bathed Love* and other epic efforts. He was
certain that his works would be recognized by
coming generations, but, at the moment, all the
editors and the publishers in the world stood

between him and his public. Hence his search for a 'congenial' occupation. And was there anything more suitable to a poet than the parrot trade? You lived in the haunts of parrots and spent your time in their company. What an opulent life for a poet! And in this luxury there was money. 'Prepared to pay Rs 10/- to Rs 100- . . .' The ten-rupee variety was not his concern. He was not going take the trouble to train a fourth-rate parrot. He was going to trade only in the hundred-rupee variety. The Ramani stamp on a parrot was going to stand for the best in parrots and nothing less. One such parrot a month and you made your hundred a month.

He had as yet very vague notions of the parrot business but he believed in luck and intuition. Sometimes he sat down, pen in hand, with next to nothing in his head, and at the end of three hours the sheets of paper before him would be filled with a poetic drama or a wonderful sonnet sequence. How was it done? Through luck and intuition. And the same qualities were now going to pull him through the parrot business.

He answered the advertisement. Two days later he received a letter from one Mr Madusudhan asking him to see him at his residence in Saidapet. Ramani had no idea where parrots were available nor did he know of any parrot that could talk. All the same he had answered in order to study the parrot market.

He inscribed on a blank visiting card 'T.T.T. Ramani Parrots Ltd.' and started for Saidapet. He took the electric train. He found his way to Mr Madusudhan's bungalow and sent his card in. He was ushered into a hall where a fat man, sitting cross-legged on thick piles of cushions, welcomed him. 'Ah, take that chair, Mr T.T.T. Ramani,' Mr Madusudhan said. 'For years I have been trying to secure a decent parrot. All sorts of persons promised and disappointed me. I grew desperate and advertised.'

'Ah, is that so?' Ramani asked warmly.

'I was able to get parrots that could only say "How are you?", "Ranga, Ranga", "Who is there?" and such other nonsense, but not one that could utter a prayer.'

'What a pity!' Ramani said sympathetically. 'What a pity that we didn't know each other before. We specialize in religious parrots. I am the trainer in our firm you know.' He added as an afterthought, 'I have engaged four Brahmin priests in my department to coach the parrots.'

'Ah, how cursed am I that I did not know you before. How is that I don't see your advertisements anywhere?'

'We don't advertise. We have our select clientele and we usually do not take up extra business.'

'How is it that I have not had the pleasure of meeting your parrots anywhere in these parts?'

'Our religious parrots sell steadily in Benares and in a few pilgrim centres in the north, but the bulk of our business is in South Africa and the Federation of Malay States.'

Ramani was offered fruits and coffee. 'I should like to see your farm sometime,' Mr Madusudhan said.

'With pleasure,' Ramani said. 'But I am going up north for a few weeks on business. As soon as I return I will take you round our parrot farm.' He had a sudden inspiration and added, 'I have trained a few parrots in the business line too. They just quote prices and so on and are suitable for business houses. I have some for coffee hotels too. These just reel off the menu. All labour-saving devices. In these hustling times they ought to be very valuable. These business-line parrots save the energy of the shop assistants who have to repeat the same thing over and over again to every customer who comes in. All the saved-up energy could be utilized by the principal of a firm for more productive purposes. This is the place of the parrot in modern economy. Would you care to see our business parrots?'

'No,' said Mr Madusudhan. 'They aren't useful to me. I have retired from business. My thoughts are with God now. I want a bird that will be filling my house with holy sounds. I want a bird that will utter *slokas*. I am prepared to pay even one-hundred-and-fifty rupees for such a parrot. Please tell me when I can come for my parrot.'

'I can't say definitely when I can have one ready for you. I have some advance bookings on hand. In about two months I think I can meet your order.'

In fairness to Ramani it must be said that he had not intended to lie. He had gone there in order to understand the conditions of the parrot market but in his talk with Mr Madusudhan his imagination caught fire and he saw Parrots Ltd. gradually revealed to him in all its detail of organization. It was more a loud brown study than downright falsehood.

Ramani went home and definitely made up his mind to start the parrot business. His first transaction would be with Mr Madusudhan. He would devote all his waking hours in the next two months to training a parrot for Mr Madusudhan. The labour would be worth Rs 150. In course of time, with a little practice, he could have a parrot a month ready for sale. As for customers he was confident that he could find at least one Madusudhan a month in this wide world. Certain other details of the work bothered him. Once a customer got his parrot the transaction was done with as long as the parrot lived. What was the normal longevity of a parrot? Probably ten years. So it meant that normally a customer would not return for ten years. For a moment Ramani wondered if it would be wise to earn the confidence of his customers' servants and bribe them to leave the cages open . . .

The instinct that leads the cow to the grass and the fly to the sugar bowl was responsible for taking Ramani to Moore Market, and there one Kandan became his friend. Kandan had just been loitering around when he noticed Ramani making eager enquiries at the stalls. He introduced himself to him: 'Master in need of a parrot?'

'Yes.'

'What sort of parrot?'

'A parrot that can be trained to talk. Have you one?' 'Years ago when I was in the army I had a parrot. It could give commands for the troop drill. It was our best companion at Mespot; but my officer took a fancy to it and I gave it to him . . . I know where parrots are to be had and I can get you one if you want . . .' In the course of an hour or two, squatting on a patch of grass in front of Moore Market and talking, a great friendship developed between Ramani and Kandan. They came to an agreement. Kandan was to secure a young parrot immediately and train it. He was to deliver the parrot complete in two months and receive ten rupees in return. In due course he would be employed in Parrots Ltd., on a salary of fifty rupees a month. Before they parted for the evening a rupee had changed hands.

Two days later Kandan came to Ramani's house and told him that he had purchased a young parrot from some villager. Thereafter he dropped in frequently to keep Ramani informed of the

physical and mental progress of the parrot.
Sometimes he demanded an odd anna or two for
buying certain secret drugs essential for the
parrot's throat. In a few days he came to
announce that the parrot was just able to repeat
'Krishna, Krishna' and also the first two lines of
a prayer to God Subramanya. Ramani was quite
pleased with Kandan's work and promised to
give him five rupees more than the agreed
amount. Even then the balance would be in his
favour. He drafted the balance sheet thus.

Expenditure

	Rs	A	P
Cost of parrot ..	1	0	0
Special throat drugs ..	1	8	0
Trainer's fee ..	15	0	0
Total ..	17	8	0

Income

	Rs	A	P
Selling price of trained parrot ..	150	0	0
Profit ..	132	8	0

Ramani clamoured so much to see the parrot
that one dark night Kandan brought a cage
with a heavy piece of cloth wrapped round it.

'I say I can't see anything, take away the
cloth,' Ramani said. 'It can't be done,' Kandan

replied firmly. 'The bird is still young. It will die of paralysis if it is allowed to open its eyes on these new surroundings all of a sudden.'

'But how am I to see the bird?' Ramani asked.

'You may peep through this chink if you like.'

Ramani lifted the cage and was about to hold it against the light. 'Ah, don't do it,' Kandan screamed. 'Do you want to blind it for life?'

Ramani put down the cage. He applied his eyes to a very small opening in the cloth wrapping and said, 'I see some faint shape inside but I can't say whether it is a ball of wool or a chicken or a parrot.' At this Kandan looked so hurt that Ramani felt sorry for allowing these frivolous words to cross his lips, and apologized. Ramani asked why the bird was not fluttering its wings inside the cage. Kandan explained that he had tied its wings to its sides; otherwise there was danger of its wasting all its energy in fluttering its wings; every ounce of its energy had to be conserved for cultivating its voice. Ramani desired to hear the voice of the parrot. Kandan declared that at nights parrots could not be made to talk.

'Well, well. You may deliver it to me in working order on the thirteenth of next month.'

'Certainly, master,' Kandan said. 'It will be the most garrulous parrot one would ever wish to meet.'

'Mere garrulity is not enough,' Ramani said. 'It must be the most religious-minded parrot.'

On the twelfth of the following month Kandan brought a green parrot in a cage. It was a rakish looking, plump bird. The sight of it sent a thrill through Ramani. He had not thought that an ambition could be so readily realized. A small thread was tied round the beak of the parrot. Kandan explained, 'It is better that you keep it tied till you reach your customer's place. Otherwise the rascal will talk all the way and gather a crowd behind you.' Ramani insisted on examining the full accomplishments of the parrot now. Kandan requested Ramani to go out of the room for a few minutes and he would untie the thread and coax the bird. Of course it could be made to talk even in Ramani's presence but then it might take time, and he (Kandan) would now have to go and attend on his aunt, who was lying in a serious condition in General Hospital. He could coax the bird much quicker if Ramani would oblige him by going out. Ramani went out of the room. Presently he heard the gruff voice of Kandan coaxing the bird. And then the parrot uttered in a melodious voice, 'Krishna, Krishna.' 'Rama, Rama,' and the first two lines of a prayer to God Subramanya. As soon as Ramani re-entered the room, Kandan said, 'I have tied the thread again. As soon as you take him over to your customer's place snip off the thread with scissors. If you give him a red, ripe chilli he will be very friendly with you in an hour or two, and then you can coax him to utter the holy sounds.'

'Right, thanks. Do you want your money now?'

'H'm, yes,' said Kandan. 'I have to buy some medicine for my aunt.'

Ramani took his savings-bank account, went to the Vepery Post Office, bled his account white, and handed fifteen rupees to Kandan. The old clerk at the counter looked at Ramani sourly. The old clerk looked on Ramani's recent withdrawals with marked disfavour. Ramani said apologetically, 'I will come back in the evening and deposit one-hundred-and-thirty rupees.'

Kandan took leave of Ramani and hurried away to his aunt's bedside.

'Ah! Ah! come in, Mr Ramani,' said Mr Madusudhan as soon as Ramani appeared in Saidapet with a parrot in hand. 'I am so happy that you have brought the parrot. Really! Really! Or am I dreaming? Ah, you are correct to the hour.'

'In business, punctuality is everything,' said Ramani. Mr Madusudhan took him in. He inspected the cage with delight; and asked again and again if the holy names of gods were going to echo through his halls thenceforth. 'Does the bird really utter the names of Krishna and Rama?'

'Absolutely,' Ramani replied. 'It was trained

under my personal supervision.'

They sat on a sofa with the cage between them. Ramani took a pair of scissors and sniped off the thread tied round the beak. He took out a ripe chilli and gave it to the bird. It ate the chilli gratefully.

Ramani said, 'Since this is a new place it will take about half an hour for him to open his mouth.'

'Let him. Let him take his own time,' said Mr Madusudhan. Ramani thrust another chilli into the cage and the parrot attacked it with vigour. They watched it for sometime, and then Mr Madusudhan asked 'Will you have your cheque immediately or sometimes later?'

Ramani was not used to such questions. He grinned awkwardly and said, 'Oh, I have not brought the receipt book.'

'It does not matter. You can send the receipt later on.'

'May we hope for another order from you?'

It was at this stage that the shrieking question was asked in Tamil! 'Are you mad?' It was followed by the command 'Get out, you fool!' Ramani looked at the cage in consternation. The parrot had eaten all the chilli and was now in a loquacious mood. He chuckled quietly, and winked at Ramani before saying in lucid English, 'Hands up or I shoot! You son of a . . .' Mr Madusudhan choked as he asked, 'Is this the kind of holy sound that is going to fill my house?' He glared at Ramani.

'There is some mistake,' mumbled Ramani. He suddenly rose and fled, leaving the cage behind. He did not stop to turn and look till he reached his house in Vepery.

Two days later a small advertisement in a paper said: 'LOST: a green parrot in cage kept in front of the house. Finder will be rewarded . . .' Ramani wondered for a moment if it would be worth his while to put this person on the track of the parrot. But he realised that he might be hauled up for theft. For sometime he lived in terror of being hunted down by Mr Madusudhan, but fortunately the visiting card he had left behind contained only his name and not his address.

The Legend on the Wall

by
M.N. Srinivas

Kirnelli is a small, sleeply village on the banks of the Hemavati. The river there is broad, deep and slow, and infested with crocodiles. A crumbling temple stands on the edge of the river, and during monsoons it is half-submerged in floods. The floods have smoothened the stones of the temple, and dark lichen coats the walls, and plants have flourished in their crannies. A very old man, almost bent double with age, is priest at the temple. He performs some kind of puja every evening, and the ringing of the sonorous bells which accompanies the puja reminds you, to your discomfort, of a world that is dying and of a world that is being born, and the clash between the two.

The village folk will tell you that somewhere in the temple, underground, is hidden a great amount of gold, which is guarded by the temple cobra. They will also tell you that only the priest has seen the sacred cobra, and that on Friday evenings, it drinks the milk kept for it, and departs only after the priest has waved *arathi* before it.

The temple, as I told you, is decaying. Its outer wall to the right of the door is covered over with writing, close and illegible, and part of the writing lies under lichen. I had wondered whenever I visited Kirnelli, what the writing might be. I wanted to ask the priest, but I never had the opportunity of meeting him at leisure.

It was evening, and the sun stood poised over the Hemavati like a flaming disc. The river was red with its reflection. The huge, sacred peepul stood by the temple like a guard. Glow-worms twinkled like gems in the hedge on the other bank. The world about me waited in a hushed silence to receive the goddess of the night. And in harmony with the hour the temple bell rang.

I went down the steps and sat on a river-step, intending to do nothing but receive the thoughts and impressions that chose to stray into my mind, just as the evening sky gives itself up to any colour that chooses to splash itself on it.

I had not been sitting there long when I

heard the banging of the temple doors, the grating of the key in the lock, and the tap-tap of a stick over the steps. I looked up and saw the priest coming down towards me.

It was a perfect evening and I did not need anyone to complete my enjoyment of it. My head was pleasantly dizzy with the beauty about me. There was a warmth in my veins and I felt as if I had drunk a mild wine.

The priest sat by my side and began. 'You know it is Friday?'

'Yes,' I replied, a little sullenly.

'But the cobra didn't come to drink the milk.'

'Perhaps it's dead,' I replied caustically.

'Dead'? He stared at me incredulously. 'Dead? You believe that the *nag* will die?' He broke into a laugh. I didn't like his laughter. Darkness had enfolded the world in its arms, the river swished along its way, and the toothless old man laughed unearthily.

'Cobras die.'

'But not the temple *nag*. It was there when the temple sprang into existence one night, thousands of years ago, at the bidding of Iswara . . . I know why it hasn't come.'

'Why?' I asked.

'A *Holeya* (untouchable) must be about here.'

'What has a *Holeya* to do with it?' I felt irritated.

'What—don't you know the tale on the wall?'

'No.'

'That explains it. Now listen.'

'It was in the year, I don't know . . . a few hundred years ago,' he began. Ten miles to the east of Kirnelli, on the other bank of the Hemavati, stood Kusumapura, capital of the Palyegar, Malle Gowda. Malle Gowda ruled with an iron hand, and his name was a terror to people for miles around. Even now, the mention of Malle Gowda's name sends our children to bed. But he was a just ruler though severe, and he inspired loyalty in his servants and soldiers.

Kirnelli was a more prosperous village then, about twenty Brahmin families inhabiting it. Those Brahmins—don't think they were like their descendants today, atheists, smokers, and drunkards. They were all great devotees of God, spending the entire day in worship and meditation. A curse from them would reduce a kingdom to ashes. Malle Gowda had a great respect for them, and granted them tax-free lands. They lived at the western end of the village, far away from the contamination of lower castes.

Hemavati here is full of crocodiles, and in those days people dared not go to the river even to take drinking water. A crocodile with more than usual daring dragged away my grandfather's brother from the river steps. The Brahmins had a well of their own very near their houses. Even today you may come across it, though it is choking with mud and weeds.

Do you see that hillock far away on the west and the old tower on its crest? That hillock is about thirty miles from here, and in those days it was of great military importance. A few *Holeyas* watched at the tower and reported if anything was wrong.

Kencha, the chief *Holeya* watchman, resting comfortably on his bed in the tower one noon, was shocked to find a number of men marching along from the western plains. He was shocked because it was the first time that any army had dared to show itself in the day. He understood that the enemy had counted on the vigil being relaxed in the noon. Ah, they were clever—and daring!

Kencha was a strong man, and he was the best runner in the kingdom of Malle Gowda. But the night-long vigil had drained his strength, and the noonday sun tired him very soon. Sweat streamed down his face. He panted for breath. He was thirsty. He felt he could drink pots of water. A coconut palm in the distance tempted him and so did a pot adorning a toddy-palm, but as I told you, Kencha had a great sense of duty. He wanted to reach the chief soon and tell him the news.

Kencha ran. The thirst was unendurable. And he knew that there was no tank or well till he reached Kirnelli. But he could not drink at the Brahmin well in Kirnelli. The river Hemavati was his only hope and he was still five miles from it.

Anyone in Kencha's place would have rested for a while under a roadside tree. But Kencha, as I said, had a great sense of duty—even though he was a *Holeya*.

At last he was a trumpet's distance from the Brahmin well. He decided, unable to bear the thirst, to beg water from the Brahmins. But supposing an angry Brahmin cursed him? Kencha was afraid of a Brahmin's curse. Did not Malle Gowda himself lose a son because of a Brahmin's curse?

He saw a woman at the well. This was an odd hour for drawing water. The gods were kind to him. He was within a stone's throw from the well, and the woman had filled two huge vessels with water. She took one big vessel, placed it on her left waist, and reached out for the second. But on second thoughts she decided to leave it there for the time being. He shouted 'Oh, mother!' The woman didn't hear.

Kencha reached the well with only one impulse in the world: to empty the vessel into his mouth. He waited for the woman to come out. He waited for what seemed to him ages. He was thirsty beyond endurance. Suddenly a strange courage possessed him. It was as if the Devil had entered his soul. He picked up the Brahmin vessel and drank it off.

At that moment the woman came out. She was stunned at first. She thought she was dreaming—a *Holeya* drinking from her vessel! Then she sent forth a shriek. The men rushed out. A terrible anger seized them. What were the times coming to? Could the *Kaliyuga* be as sinful as that?

Ranga Bhatta, my grandfather, was the heftiest man in Malle Gowda's kingdom. He was a wrestler and his strength was prodigious. He picked up a brick and hurled it at Kencha.

Kencha yelled as the brick caught him in the calf. He threw down the vessel and ran.

An angry crowd of Brahmins pursued him through the streets of Kirnelli. Kencha ran to save his dear life, and this very fear imparted to his legs extraordinary swiftness; otherwise he could not have run faster than Ranga Bhatta. The crowd was gradually getting nearer. Kencha became desperate. He suddenly realized that he should make a supreme, final effort and reach the temple. He would be safe. No one would attack him there. He swiftly changed his direction.

Now his pursuers also realized that Kencha was heading for the temple and they resolved to prevent him from doing it.

Kencha won the race narrowly. Gasping and sweating, he reached the temple wall, and vaulted over it. He fell clumsily in a heap in the courtyard, scrambled to his feet, and staggered on to the inner door. His last bit of strength was now spent. His heavy legs could not be moved. He fell prostrate before the inner door.

The Brahmins were now doubly incensed:

not only was their vessel defiled, but also their temple. But they were helpless. They could not beat him inside the temple.

Suddenly they all heard a great groan. Ranga Bhatta leaped over the wall and ran in. He was just in time to see the tail of the temple *nag*, disappearing into a hole in the wall. The divine *nag* had punished Kencha.

The dying Kencha whispered to Ranga Bhatta: 'I saw a horde of men moving towards Kirnelli from the west. Convey the news to the chief.' And the next moment he was dead.

Those were righteous days, not like the times we live in. But even now the Iswara in this temple is feared by men, and that is why Kirnelli has never suffered from a famine. Even today the *nag* will not drink milk if a *Holeya* happens to be about. The *nag* is sure to kill the sinful *Holeya* who has dared to come near the temple even though he may climb and hide himself in the tallest tower on earth. Did you see any *Holeya*?

* * *

I got up, I fear, a little abruptly. I hated the drivel I had been forced to listen to. It irritated me. I walked away in the direction of the village without replying. Presently, the irritation passed away, and I saw the old man in his true setting. He was born to a narrow tradition and inherited beliefs, and I knew, he would die with his

beliefs all intact. A narrow and contented life—
enviable—though I would not be in his position
for anything.

As I walked I wondered how the Brahmin
would feel if he learnt the fact that he had been
all along talking to a *Holeya* or rather a *Holeya*
in khaki, a Bachelor of Arts, and the Assistant
Superintendent of Police in Kundur State. The
strength of his belief would only increase, because
the *nag* chose to keep away. He would dip many
times in the icy cold Hemavati to wash away the
contamination of sitting by the side of a *Holeya*.

Under the Bo Tree

by
K. Narasimha Murthy

(This article is an outcome of reading Mr G.P. Raja Ratnam's Kannada renderings from Pali of *Milinda Prasne* and the greater part of the *Tripitaka*. I am grateful to him for his kind permission to translate extracts from his renderings.)

I

It was in the sixth century before Christ that the Buddha lived and taught the principles of his faith; but his teachings remained only on the tongues of the Buddhists till the first century when they were written down; and they form the *Tripitaka*, the scriptures of Buddhism. Of these the first two *Pitakas*, the *Vinaya* and the *Sutta*, combine profound philosophy with poetic grandeur. Like other prophets of the world, the Buddha used numerous similes to enhance the clarity and beauty of his teachings.

He refrained from elucidating the more abstract and abstruse problems as they did not tend towards the eradication of the misery in the world. This idea is strikingly brought out in the following simile from the *Sutta Pitaka*:

'Malunkyaputra! A man is deeply pierced by an envenomed arrow. His relatives and friends fetch a physician who can cure wounds caused by arrows.

'Suppose he then asks the physician, "Is the person who struck me a Kshatriya, a Brahmin, a Vaisya, or a Sudra? What is his name, and what his lineage? Is he tall, short or of middle height? Is he black, dark or golden of complexion? From which village, fortress or city did he come? Was his bow of a pliant variety or of a hard one? Did its string come from the *arka* plant, the *samstha* grass, the *maruva* fibre or the tree whose leaves exude milk? Is the stem of this arrow of *kachha* grass or the *ropima* shaft? Are the feathers at its end from the owl, the *kanka* bird, the *kalala* bird, the peacock or the bird known as *sithilahanu*? Has this sinew which I see around the stem of this arrow been obtained from the cow, the buffalo, the deer or the ape? Is this arrow of the *kharuppa* variety of the *vaikanda*, of the *naracha*, of the *vathsadantha*, or of the *karavira*? I will not have this arrow removed until I know these facts." If he puts the physician questions in this way, he will die even before they are answered.

'Similarly, Malunkyaputra! "Is the world enduring, or is it ephemeral? Has this world an end, or is it endless? Are the soul and the body one, or are they different? Will the Enlightened one exist after death, or will he not? Is there rebirth to the Enlightened one, or is he free from it? Until these doubts are clarified, I will not pursue celibacy taught by the Lord." If anyone says so, he will die even before they are clarified.'

II

Such similes as these are not sufficient and the Buddha also used parables which are in a way expanded similes, but which not only possess the charm of short stories but with their human appeal and detailing of circumstances coincide more with practical life, and are to that extent more effectual in their influence. The Buddha attained Enlightenment after a number of births in which he made himself perfect in the practice of the great virtues, and whenever he had to teach these virtues, he recounted how in his past births he had developed them. These birth-tales of *Jathakas* occur in the last of the five divisions of the *Sutta Pitaka* and their combined wisdom and charm are illustrated in the following example, depicting the power of knowledge.

Long ago, when Brahmadatta reigned in

Varanasi, the future Buddha took birth in the womb of his chief queen.

On the day the child was to be named, the king and the queen invited eight hundred Brahmins, gave them all they desired and having satisfied them, questioned them about the future of the child. The Brahmins observed the wealth of marks of good fortune, and said, 'O, King, your son is very fortunate. He will ascend the throne after you. He will acquire knowledge of the five weapons, demonstrate their use and be the foremost king in India.' Upon these words, the child was named Panchayudha Kumara.

When he grew to years of discretion and was sixteen, the king called him and said, 'You must now acquire knowledge.'

'From whom?' asked the son.

The father replied, 'From the teacher in the city of Takshasila, in Gandhara. His fame has spread in all directions.' He placed a thousand gold coins in the boy's hand, saying, 'Give this to the teacher as his portion.'

The son went to Takshasila, acquired knowledge, received the five weapons from his teacher, saluted him, and leaving Takshasila, set out for Varanasi, wielding the five weapons.

On the way was a forest ruled by a demon who was known from his intertwined hair as Slesharoma. When the future Buddha was about to enter the forest, he was stopped by people and warned against entering it and falling into the hands of Slesharoma. 'He kills,' they said, 'whomsoever he sees'. But the future Buddha, fearless like a lion of gleaming mane, did enter the forest.

He had reached the middle of the wood when the demon appeared before him. He was as tall as the palmyra tree. His head was as huge as a house. His eyes were as wide as a vessel. His nose was like a hawk's; and there were moles all over his stomach and all his limbs were blue.

He fixed his eye on the boy and cried, 'Whither do you keep going? Stop, you are my prey.'

'I have entered the forest,' replied the boy, 'after serious thought. You approach me with arrogance, but I will shoot this arrow dipped in poison and you will bite the dust.' When he shot the arrow, dipped in deadly poison, it got entangled in the demon's hair, and though he shot fifty more arrows, the demon's hair caught them all.

The demon shook off the arrows and drew near the boy. Nothing daunted, the boy struck the demon with his sword. The sword which was three and thirty inches long got stuck in the demon's hair. The boy struck him again with his spear and then with his spiked mace, but they suffered the same fate.

'O demon,' shouted the boy, 'have you not heard of my king Panchayudha Kumara? When I entered your forest I did not do so relying on my bow and other weapons. I entered relying on myself. I will now shatter you to bits.' So threatening, he struck the demon with his right hand, and, when that caught, with his left. When that also stuck, he hit him with his right foot, then with his left, and charged on him with his head, but all of them stuck. Though he was thus caught in five nets at five places and hung by them, he was yet fearless and unperturbed.

The demon observed that the boy did not tremble in the least. 'This is a lion among men,' he thought, 'I have slain many a man on this road but never met such a one. I wonder what makes him so fearless!' Hesitating to eat him, he asked. 'How is it you do not fear death?'

'Why should I fear death?' replied the future Buddha. 'For a man once born, death once is inevitable. Besides, I bear in my stomach my last weapon, the diamond sword. You can devour me but cannot digest it. On the contrary, it will cut you up from within into pieces. Thus, both of us will be destroyed. This keeps me fearless.' The future Buddha was referring to the weapon of knowledge which was within him.

'This boy utters truth,' thought the demon, and shrinking from death, he set the boy free and said, 'You are a lion among men. I will not devour you. You have escaped my hands as the moon escapes from the planet, Rahu. Go away and delight the circle of your friends and relations.'

'That I will do, and shortly,' replied the future Buddha. 'You sinned in the past and are born a devourer of blood and flesh. If you continue to redden your hands with blood, you will pass from darkness to darkness. But you cannot sin since you have seen me now. Slaughter of living beings results in a rebirth in hell in the form of a beast or ghost or giant, and if he is born a man his life will be cut short.' Thus, and in other ways, the future Buddha enlightened him on the harvest of misery which results from evil conduct, and on the happiness which springs from good deeds. Having subdued him thus, he bade him be in that forest and accept the sacrifices the people offered, making him thus the deity of that forest. Then he emerged from the woods and informed the people of all that happened.

Then, wielding the five weapons, he reached Varanasi and saw his parents. After them, he ruled the kingdom justly, performed deeds of merit, and after his death passed on to enjoy the fruits of his actions.

There is another tale which has a special significance in the modern world, with commercialism exploiting scientific knowledge.

When Brahmadatta reigned in Varanasi, there lived in a certain village a Brahmin who knew a spell called *Vaidarbha*. If one uttered it when the stars were in a favourable position, there would be a rain of seven kinds of gems.

The future Buddha was then a student of the Brahmin.

Once, the Brahmin was travelling with his student from his village to a neighbouring kingdom. On the way there was a forest infested with five hundred robbers. When they caught a pair of persons, it was their habit to send one of them to fetch the ransom.

When the Brahmin and the future Buddha fell into their hands, they sent the latter to bring the ransom. Before leaving his teacher the future Buddha bowed to him, and said, 'Do not fear. I will return in a couple of days. But the stars will reach their auspicious position this night. Whatever happens, please do not utter the spell. If you do, you will be destroyed by these five hundred robbers.' So advising him, he left.

At sunset, the robbers bound the Brahmin, hand and foot and threw him on the ground. At that moment the moon rose in the east. Observing the arrival of the stars to the required position, the Brahmin thought within himself, 'Why should I endure this distress? All that I need do is to call down the rain of gems. I will hand over the wealth to the robbers and go my way in freedom.' Accordingly, he called the robbers and asked them why they had captured him.

'To make money,' they replied.

'If you want money, unbind me swiftly, let me bathe; provide me with dry clothes, rub me with sandal paste, adorn me with flowers, and leave me standing.'

The robbers obeyed, and he uttered the spell at the auspicious moment and looked up at the sky. Instantly, there was a downpour of gems from the sky. The robbers gathered the gems, and set out with the Brahmin behind them.

On the way another set of five hundred robbers captured these robbers. The first band asked, 'Why do you capture us?' The second replied, 'To make money.' The first band said, 'If you want money, take this Brahmin. He can bring down a rain of gems. We have obtained these gems with his aid.'

The second band freed the first and commanded the Brahmin to call down a rain of gems.

'I am prepared to do it,' answered the Brahmin. 'But you will have to wait for a year. My spell can work only when the stars are in a favourable position.'

The robbers became angry. 'O wicked Brahmin,' they cried. 'You called down a rain of gems just now for these robbers and you want *us* to wait for another year!' So saying, they killed him, and overtaking the first set of robbers, killed them and took possession of their gems. Then, they started quarrelling among themselves; and splitting into equal divisions, they fought against each other. In a short time only one on either side was left.

They gathered the gems in a heap. One sat on guard with his sword, and the other went to the village to fetch food. When the latter returned with the food, the guard, desiring to have all the game to himself, struck him with his sword and killed him. But the same desire had animated the other also, with the result that he had poisoned the food. The guard ate the food and died.

About three days later, the future Buddha returned with the ransom. But what met his eyes was the mutilated body of his teacher. Surmising the cause of his death, he prepared a pyre, burnt the corpse and worshipped the ashes with wild flowers. Walking further, he saw the ground covered with the corpses of robbers, and nearby, the dead bodies of the last two bandits, and beside them the heaps of gems.

And then he proclaimed the truth, saying, 'He, who like my teacher, cannot control himself and without discretion invokes a rain of gems for unmeriting persons, will not only destroy himself but destroy others also.' These words echoed through the forest, and the gods expressed their approval. Then the future Buddha had the gems brought home and distributed the wealth to the poor. When his life ended, he departed to occupy his vacant seat in heaven.

After the *Pitakas*, but before the commentaries upon them by writers like Buddha Ghosha, there was produced a work of great interest. This was *Milinda Prasne*, worshipped as much as the *Pitakas* themselves. It is in the form of a dialogue between King Milinda, supposed to have been the Menander of history, and Nagasena, a great Buddhist sage. The mode of discussion is defined in the beginning, and follows Buddha's aim of allowing the devotee complete independence of mind, and convincing him rather than dictating to him:

'Revered Nagasena,' said the king. 'Will you discuss things with me?'

'O King, I will converse with you if you speak as a seeker of knowledge. I will not, if you speak as a king.'

'How do they speak, who are seekers after knowledge?'

'O King, in the course of discussion, they will imply things, they will explain things; they will point out errors, they will acknowledge their errors; they will define what the nature of each thing is, they will define what the nature of each thing is not. Therefore, the seekers after knowledge are never angered. This is how they speak.'

'How do kings speak?'

'Kings in discussions make assertions. If anyone opposes them, they fine him or punish him in other ways. This is how they speak.'

'Revered Nagasena, I will speak as a seeker of knowledge, not as a king. Let the revered one speak as freely as before the inmates of the hermitages. Let there not be a vestige of fear.'

'Agreed, O king!' replied Nagasena with delight.

Again, the nature of inquiry is thus explained.

'Revered Nagasena, what is the nature of inquiry?'

'Striking again and again.'

'Will you give a simile?'

'O King, if a bronze vessel is struck on the ground it is followed by a sound which gradually takes shape. Concentration is to be understood as striking the vessel, inquiry as the reverberation.'

'You are wise, revered Nagasena.'

There comes an expression of a conception of time, advanced beyond its material aspect and become truly subjective:

'Revered Nagasena, how long is it since you became a *Bikshu*?'

'O King, I have been seven years a Bikshu.'

'How can you have been seven years? Is seven you? Is seven a number?'

The shadow of king Milinda, his figure embellished with decorations, showed both on the floor and in the water in the vase.

Then the long-lived Nagasena said, 'O King, your shadow is seen both on the floor and in the water in the vase. Are you the king? Or is the shadow the king?'

'Revered Nagasena, it is I who am the king. The shadow is not the king. It only depends on one and acts accordingly.'

'Similarly, seven is the number of years. It is not I. It is dependent on me like the shadow and acts accordingly.'

'Both the occurring of the question to my mind and its elucidation by you are alike brilliant, revered Nagasena!'

On another occasion, the king asks:

'Is there such a thing as time, revered Nagasena?'

'Some "time" exists, some does not.'

'Which exists? Which does not?'

'O King "time" does not exist for those whose sensations are buried in the past, are lost, are ended, are changed. But for those who execute activities which have consequences, who are of a nature to do deeds which bear fruit and who are of a nature to cause rebirth in any other way, for these "time" does exist. It exists for those who die and are reborn elsewhere; it does not exist for those who die and are not born again elsewhere. For souls which attain the final liberation, time is non-existent.'

'You are wise, revered Nagasena.'

No idea is more characteristic of Buddhism than the stress laid on the potency of action in the making of an individual. This is brought out in the following beautiful dialogue, beautiful in its idea, approach, and manner of writing:

'Revered Nagasena,' said the king. 'All men are not alike or equally placed: some are short-lived, some live long; some are victims of disease, some escape them lightly; some are uncouth, some are handsome, some feeble, some strong; some are wealthy, some indigent; some are born in a low caste and family, some in high caste and family: some have no sense, some have profound insight. Why is there this inequality?'

'O King,' replied Nagasena, 'Some trees are sour, some are saltish, some pungent, some bitter, some astringent and some sweet. Why are they not all alike?'

'Because they have sprung from seeds of different sorts I suppose.'

'Similarly, O King, people are not alike; they are dissimilar, as you observed, because their actions have been different.'

'You are wise, revered Nagasena.'

If a man performs virtuous acts and develops great qualities like friendliness, generosity, truthfulness, insight, and restraint, to perfection, he will overcome misery in this life and will be released from the round of rebirths hereafter. For such a man death holds no terrors. The following passage reveals this attitude of Buddhism to death.

'Revered Nagasena, why does not he who feels the pangs of grief seek his final liberation in death?'

'O King, an *Arhata* does not desire death and court it. Nor does he detest it and flee from it. An *Arhata* does not pluck a fruit which is unripe. He will wait for it to mature. Revered Sariputra asserts:

> *I will not bow down to death, I will not*
> *bow down to life;*
> *I await the hour as a servant awaits his*
> *wages.*
> *I will not bow down to death, I will not*
> *bow down to life;*
> *I await the time with my memory*
> *unsleeping.*

'You are wise, revered Nagasena.'

Even as early as Nagasena's time the humanity of the Buddha was beginning to be overlaid by divine and mystic characteristics. But this description of the magic body of a super-man like the Buddha is exquisitely suggestive of the mystery of a great soul's birth in a mediocre world.

'Revered Nagasena, did the Buddha possess the three and thirty marks of the highest man? Did he shine with the eighty secondary signs? Was his complexion of gold? Was there a halo its radius the length of an arm around him?'

'Yes, the Lord possessed them.'

'Were his parents possessed of them?'

'They were not.'

'But a child must resemble either its mother or her relations, or its father or his relations?'

'Does the hundred-petalled lotus exist?'

'It exists.'

'Where is it born?'

'In mire, and it has its refuge in water.'

'Is the lotus like the mire in colour or scent or honey?'

'It is not.'

'Or like water in colour or scent or honey?'

'It is not.'

'Similarly, O King, the Buddha possessed the characteristics you mention though his parents were not possessed of them.'

'You are wise, revered Nagasena.'

There is but a trace here of the miraculous, but, pure even from such a trace, the passage which follows describes with one of the grandest of similes the passing away of one of the greatest souls from this world.

'Revered Nagasena, does the Buddha exist?'

'Yes, the Lord exists.'

'Revered Nagasena, is it possible to point at him and say "Here is the Buddha!?"

'The Lord attained his final liberation. It is not possible to point at him and say, "Here is the Lord."'

'Why is it not?'

'Is it possible to point at a flame which is extinguished in the midst of a blazing fire, and say, "Here is the flame?"'

'No, the flame is ended. It has disappeared.'

'Similarly, the Lord has attained his final liberation. It is not possible to point at the Lord who has disappeared and say, "Here is the

Lord." But it is possible to show the Lord in his aspect of righteousness which he taught and in which he survives.'

'You are wise, revered Nagasena.'

The Vendor of Sweets

by

K.V. Jagannathan

*(Translated from Tamil by
Srimati K. Savitri)*

He was a vendor of sweets. He had his own peculiar method of advertising and doing business. He never depended upon other for help. He worked hard all alone.

I speak of Munisamy—the man who sold sweets. His customers were children, the future citizens of the world. How they were attracted by the sight of him as he went singing his song and ringing his iron bell!

He knew a lot about schools though not about reading or writing. He could tell you off-hand that two hundred children were studying in that red-painted school facing west in Sankaran Chetti Street and that a fourth of them were girls.

At the stroke of nine in the morning he would stand in front of the school with his tray of sweets. Till about eleven the sale would be brisk. After that he moved off to other places. The sun might beat down ever so fiercely; but he did not mind it. Even when the sweets became sticky in the heat, his business never slackened.

At five minutes to one in the afternoon he again presented himself near the school. Between one and two, the lunch hour for children—he did good business, and at two-thirty went away to sell in the streets. He would go round every nook and corner of the town and try his luck and present himself again at the school at four. At four-thirty the children streamed out as though they were let out of a prison, and they loved to buy a coconut or an onion sweet and suck it as they went home.

Sometimes Munisamy spent a whole day at one school. At others he visited all the schools by turns. He somehow managed to earn eight annas by the evening. They were all coppers, mostly pies, which he brought home.

Thus Munisamy found a thriving business in vending sweets. There was depression in his trade only when the holidays came. He had to wander far and wide at such times. His trade could have no rest. It might be possible only when he could give rest to his stomach!

✳ ✳ ✳

On Sundays he prepared enough sweets to last a whole week. His wife also helped him in the preparation. She earned four rupees a month by sweeping the floor and cleaning vessels in four houses. Their earnings, put together, enabled them to live a simple, peaceful life. A son was born to them.

The summer holidays commenced for the children. For a whole month and a half their merry voices were absent from those cells. The beauty of the place—its life—had vanished and with it the presence of Munisamy too ceased to haunt the place.

He hated the silence of the school. The holidays meant a sweet restful sleep for the children, but Munisamy looked upon it as death. Such days were a crisis in his life, recurring unfailingly. They seemed never to move while the other days simply flew on.

And they were the hottest days of the year. He had to wander a lot. He returned home in the evening with tired limbs and a weary spirit.

'The holidays will be over at last. Only a week more. I must borrow a little more from someone and buy sugar, gingelly, and other stuff for making cakes and sweets,' he told himself. But who would lend him money? His wife helped him. She managed to get two rupees from the mistress of one of the houses in which she worked. With this money Munisamy did some shopping.

Their boy was now two years old—an age at

which a child is apt to put all kinds of things into its mouth. Munisamy, however, would not let him touch even the little crumbs that dropped on the ground. What right had a poor child to eat sweets? 'If I allow him once, he will get into the habit and it will be a nuisance afterwards,' he argued. But could a child understand the legitimacy of his arguments?

'Papa! a sweet for me,' the little one would ask.

'You will have only a kick,' would cut in the angry voice of the father. His sweet words made other children flock round him and buy his sweets. But he hardly knew how to speak to his own child. For, the other children were his customers while this one was just a little slave born to obey his authority. Whether he actually thought so or not his hand-to-mouth existence reduced him to it.

'How you shout at a little child! What does he know?' his wife would protest.

'Go to, you ass! "A silken string indeed for the broomstick!" As if he could not do without eating sweets!'

'Have we earned anything more, though, by denying him?' she would mutter to herself.

The child would stand crying for the sweet. The sight would fill the mother's heart with pain, and enrage the father. He would not, however, raise his hand against the child. He had not descended to that level yet.

* * *

It was the re-opening day of the school. Munisamy got up early. It was like the dawn of a new year for him. He had decorated the tray with coloured paper and arranged the sweets on it.

'This is the first day. God grant that the sweets may sell well,' he prayed and applied on his forehead sacred ash. He rolled a long piece of cloth into a turban and put it on his head. He had forgotten to take out the little iron bell on the previous day. Now he took it out and placed the auspicious vermilion mark on it and on the tray.

He then swallowed a little *kanji* and went out to wash his hands. The child chose precisely that moment to approach the tray: he picked up a sweet from it, and put it into his mouth.

Munisamy saw it. 'Damn the fellow!' he cried and gave a sharp slap on the tender cheeks of the child. He then hastily took up the tray and went out of the house.

The child sank on the floor shrieking with pain. At the impact of the blow the little bit of sweet he was sucking dropped from his mouth. He screamed as though he were in the throes of death.

The mother came running, and gathered him in her arms. 'Oh! The villain! He has killed the child!' she wailed. 'Has God no eyes? Oh! My darling! Why did He will it that you should be born to this cursed woman? Your lot would have been happier even if you had been born to a scavenger. You have fallen a prey to this human beast. Surely, this is a punishment for my sins. When I took him the other day to the Mudaliar's house how that lady admired him! "He looks a very prince! Look after him carefully," she advised me. Oh! My little prince, how can that devil have the heart to beat you?' she lamented.

Meanwhile Munisamy was walking along very fast, with the tray on his head. 'The little fellow's hand has touched the sweets. It is an ill omen. Suppose it affects the sale today!' he reflected. 'I should not have hit him so hard, however, and come away, without even caring to see how he did. I shall not lose anything indeed by giving him just a little piece,' he reflected again in a different strain.

'Children ought not to have their own way in everything. Even the son of a king must learn to be obedient,' went on his thoughts in yet another strain.

'But what can the little fellow know at his age? He has done no wrong! I am so hard on him while I am selling sweets to hundreds of little children.'

Thus a multitude of thoughts rose and surged in his mind. Just as he was going along a lane, he suddenly saw a big car bearing down in his direction. He hurried to a side, when his foot stumped against a big stone and he fell headlong on the ground. The car flew past him. The sweets tray fell from his head into the gutter by the side of the road. His turban rolled away in one direction and the iron bell in another.

Munisamy got up and gave vent to his feelings freely. He picked up the turban and the iron bell, and looked for the sweets tray. The sweets were all lying in the gutter. Picking up the empty tray from the gutter he seated himself on the very stone which had sent him down prostrate. Luckily his body was uninjured, but his heart was.

The sweets—the whole lot, from which he would not allow a single bit to be removed even for his own child—lay in a heap before his very eyes, in the gutter. They were lost, irretrievably lost.

Sitting on that stone he looked into his own heart and subjected it to a thorough scrutiny.

'Alas! what a wretch I am to beat an innocent little child!' he thought mournfully. 'The sweets have all fallen into the gutter. Of what use can they be to any one now? Had I given just one to the little fellow it would have at least escaped this fate. Now God knows whether the child is alive or dead: I did hit him hard in my frenzy. Suppose he is seriously hurt . . .'

Such thoughts harassed his mind and the tears filled his eyes. He beat his head and reflected bitterly again. 'I prayed to God, applied the sacred ashes on my forehead, and all that. But I beat the child and was not aware that he was the image of that same God. Can the just

God tolerate it? Indeed, it is He that has pushed all the sweets into the gutter.'

All at once he was filled with an intense desire to go home and see his child. He got up, unrolled the turban and threw it over his shoulder and with the bell and the empty tray in his hands, he started back for home.

'Why, you have returned so soon! Have all the sweets been sold away?' his wife asked.

The child had cried itself to sleep on her lap. Munisamy saw the red marks of his fingers on the soft cheeks and also the stain of tears over them.

'The sweets were all lost in the gutter,' he said in a sad voice.

She was seized with fear. What if he should beat the child again to death thinking that the accident was due only to the child's laying his hand upon the tray! She did not wish to rouse his anger by referring to his cruelty in the morning. Accordingly she held her peace. He expected she would berate him severely. But she did nothing of the kind. Her silence went to his heart. He laid down the tray and, feeling weary and exhausted, went and sat in a corner of the room. He hardly knew what to say, neither could she venture to break the silence.

Although he remained silent outwardly, a storm raged in his heart. He felt his heart would burst if he did not say something.

'Is he sleeping?' he asked.

'Yes.'

'Did he cry very much?'

'Why do you talk about things which do not concern you?'

'Did I hit him hard?'

'Perhaps you did. What about it now?'

'Is he hurt by any chance?'

At this series of questions she burst out indignantly, 'Very fine indeed! Your coming and speaking to me like this! Why did you not straight away kill the child with a single blow? Having treated him so foully you come out now with your enquiries! Will not God make you suffer for this!' She could speak no further. She burst out weeping.

Munisamy's eyes also filled with tears. He restrained himself with some effort. 'Come now,' he said her. 'Hear me. I swear to God I will not touch the child again. I sinned and God has punished. I say, do not cry . . .' He broke into sobs. In this commotion the child woke up from its sleep and looked at them.

Munisamy got up and went to the basket in which he stored the sweets. He came back with his hands full of sweets and gave them to the child.

'My darling! From today you will have it first,' he said and kissed the cheek which he had slapped in the morning.

The child smiled. Biting the sweet he looked at his parents and burst into a laugh.

'Look at the little rogue laughing!' exclaimed Munisamy. What relief he had now! What bliss!

By kind permission of *Ananda Vikatan* of Madras.

The Waif

by
"K"

What could the little boy know of the music of Eastern lands—so strange, so weird, so full of mystery? He was so small, looking like an elfish thing. His frame was delicate, and the winter before last, a terrible one, had given him consumption. But there was fire in his eyes and pliancy in his limbs. 'Five hits at my knuckle from your marble; just come and take the game.' That was how the lazy son of an indifferent neighbour seduced poor Nanoo to play and Nanoo's marbles hit the other's knuckles rather sorely. I wondered how the boy used to play the live-long day, at the same time running various errands for all my neighbours. He scrubbed the floor in my house, gathered flowers for my neighbour, ran for the doctor, the barber, or the washerman to answer demands for them.

Very few knew how he came to be about us.
I caught him one day chasing butterflies in an
early hour when the sun shone brightly among
the trees after a night of heavy rain. Chasing
the butterflies and catching them from under
his thin garment, he let them off to chase them
once more. On another occasion, when there
was a grand festival by the waterfall on the hills
to the west of the town, I saw Nanoo busy
ringing the temple bell, scattering flowers
gathered about the garden there, and making
friends with the monkeys which ran away to the
topmost trees with coconuts and plantain fruits
left unguarded about.

Monkeys are a disreputable race. My
neighbour's child was playing with a jewel
belonging to its mother who was busy offering
flowers to the waterfall representing the Holy
Gunga. There was a scream from the child and
in a moment a monkey had abstracted the jewel
from the child, and run away to the topmost
branch of a tall tree. Perhaps the bright jewel
suggested various fancies to the thief of a
monkey. But how was the jewel, a fortune by
itself, to be recovered? Nanoo in a moment made
a weird call to the monkey, which obediently
came forward and placed the jewel in the hands
of the child.

Nobody knew whether Nanoo had any parent
living. He grew among us like any flower in the
crannies of walls. Nature nurtured him and we

did the rest. Yet the pity of it! Was he not a loafer? a street Arab who was not to be associated with the pieties of the earth?

I remember the day quite well. It was after ten in the night when the moon was full, and all the fairness of the earth came out vividly in the resplendent hour. I had arranged for a musical performance on the fiddle by a master whose fame was thrilling the whole country. The performance was over at about one in the morning. A strange pathos being everywhere, our feelings were highly strung, and some heaved sighs which ended in tears.

The next morning found us deep in our daily vocations. Nanoo had promised his help in getting me a jasmine plant of a rare kind. That day I missed the boy, and both men and boys came inquiring after him for he had something to do for every one of them. We all missed him from that day, and in course of time many had forgotten his existence. But I could never forget the poor orphan boy who came into our midst all unknown and went away, none knew whither, having made it all sunshine during his stay with us.

Years passed. One day, when it was spring time, there was a certain freshness in the air. In the usual course of rambles that morning, I stayed away beyond the usual time of returning home, for there was light in the bushes and music in the wind above. I had just reached my arms through the hedges to pluck a sunflower when a strange wave of melody reached my ears, and before me was a passer-by who sang out a stray bar of music that lay somewhere in his brain. A few yards behind him was a boy of some twelve summers with a bundle of stringed instruments clasped on to his shoulders. His hands were in the act of drawing a bow over a fiddle with but two strings. In an instant the boy had caught the vagrant tune of the passer-by and worked it out on the fiddle, and the thrill of it went through my frame and shook it.

'Nanoo,' I cried, 'what had become of you all these days? Where had you hidden yourself? Answer me, my boy! For have we not missed you?' The boy replied—a very strange boy indeed! There was none the like of him ever that I knew. How did he answer my inquiries? Having caught the tune from the wayfarer before him he crushed out of the frail frame of the instrument the wildest and the most pathetic of musical notes, and made one pant and sob for the very ecstasy of it. And it was thus some time before he could give me a reply, and then, 'Oh, sir, excuse me! My instrument will force me to forget even gratitude. I ran away from you? Why? That is a story.' And I learnt that the boy's passion for music, long hid in his heart, was roused by the famous fiddler who had played in my house some years before. The boy had run away to him and sworn that he would lay down his life to listen to that great musician. And by little service he won the heart of the master who taught him the art. Though not proficient, the boy could awake the strangest passion on the delicate wires, by his touch. And he made for sale miniature little fiddles on which little boys and girls might play. And the little boys and girls ran after him, as he drew the lead on his own; and they parted with their little cash to possess these fragile bits of wood. I asked him if the sale brought enough for him. He said, he generally got enough for his day's needs, but that people often listened to him and went away without buying an instrument. But there was no complaint in what he said. I induced him to visit us once more. And when he did so, it was quite a great event in the annals of the little village. But I knew he would not suffer himself to stay long away from his occupation, and the day came when he vanished from our midst and nobody knew where he had gone.

In the meanwhile, the great rains had failed and a great drought had parched the land and sucked out the waters. 'The earth was iron-bound, and the heavens one sheet of brass.' And on odd occasions I used to think of the poor boy, Nanoo. Could he but thrive on his odd custom, famine could never touch him. But then I knew that hunger murders love. How could he thrive now when crumbs were dearer and rarer? And my heart bled for the poor boy.

One day I was sitting in the verandah of my house. News was brought to me that Nanoo was dying even at that moment on the bank of the river. I hurried to the spot, and when I saw him with his fiddle broken by his side he was gone past all recovery. He looked a skeleton. The famine had done its work. A smile wreathed his wan lips. He dribbled out in the intervals of gasping for breath the story of his struggle against hunger, and he could not be stopped— for he knew he was dying fast. The story is soon told. The famine drove away bounty from hearths where he had lived in better times. Nobody listened to his songs, none bought his instruments. Custom failed, and he joined a famine camp where he broke stones for a public way, under a blazing sun. He wore out his heart for music; he could neither eat the poor fare of a famine camp, nor sleep after a day's cruel toil. And the consumption gave him the final blow. He ran away from the camp. He ran away to where his instrument was hidden, and played on it, till it drove him out of his mind, for the high fever was on him. He dragged himself on to our river side, thinking of us in his last moments. Oh, the last moments! And he came there to die. And he died towards six in the evening when the sun went down behind the hills. With him was buried his broken gourd of music, and the river goes on for ever, seeming to murmur in odd little splashes the story of Nanoo, the waif.

The Unveiling

by
N. Kasturi
(Translated from Kannada)

Trng . . . trng . . . trng . . . trng . . . the Baby
Ben struck four! It was less than half an hour
since it had been hung on the wall and put on
duty. I considered myself very lucky. For the
whole long previous day it had jolted with my
entire household furniture, utensils, wife and
children in a rickety bullock-cart all the way
from Holé Halli (where I was last employed) to
Nanjarajpet (where I was now transferred). It
was a journey of eighteen miles on a rugged
road in foul weather. I was pleased that the
delicate intricacies of the clock's interior had
stood the journey so well. All my other goods,
tables and chairs, were old and dilapidated; but
the clock was shining and fresh. That was the
only symbol of the Scientific Age in my humble

home, and so I prized it all the more. It was also a recent acquisition and a gift—given to me as Headmaster by the agent of a sports-goods firm.

When the clock struck, my little son, a real prodigy, I must tell you, called out 'Anna! It's time. Aren't you going to the meeting?' I couldn't, just for a moment, spot the engagement. Children have an alert brain, you see, and so the little fellow ran up, put his hand into my coat-pocket, and fetched the invitation itself! Would you believe it: the rascal was only five years and a few months old!

* * *

On the previous evening, just when our cart reached Nanjarajpet and stopped in front of my predecessor's house (I had fixed it up as my residence also) a peon appeared and asked, as if he were in charge of reception arrangements, 'Swami, who is the new Headmaster?' I answered sharply, 'Don't you see? I am the person.' I noticed a faint disappointment in his face. He handed me a letter and went away. The first thing I did on entering my new home was to make my little son read it for me. For, I had not yet recovered my spectacles from the big box. Besides, it gives the boy some training in literary style and elocution if he is made to read letters now and then . . . The letter said that Mr Bhangarappa, retired Inspector of Police, was unveiling the portrait of Mr Ramabhadrayya, late *amildar* of Nanjarajpet and founder of the Town Club. He was praised as the 'Benefactor of the Club' since he had secured from the Government free gift of a site for the 'Club aforesaid . . .'.

Certainly, it was very clever of my son to remind me of the unveiling ceremony. It was a splendid chance to see all the big townsmen in a lump. I dare not invite trouble by disregarding the first invitation that had reached me in my new sphere of work. Above all, I could not possibly appear to neglect Mr Bhangarappa. The Headmaster whom I was succeeding had been 'private tutor' to two of Mr Bhangarappa's sons on a salary of five rupees a month. He was good enough to tell me of this gold mine, and that very morning I trudged up to the bungalow of the retired Inspector of Police and placed my salutations at his feet. 'Begin your lessons tomorrow. You too may carry away the five rupees I am destined to part with . . .' he said.

Of course much of the household stuff was still lying helter-skelter and She couldn't arrange more than a fraction of it, for we were expecting an addition to the family in a week or two. But the unveiling function was very important, and I made ready to go. I tightened the turban on my brow with an extra pull on the last bit at the back; I dusted the coat with my walking stick while putting it on. And, behold! The new Headmaster stepped into the street.

I had gone ten steps or twelve when a voice from behind invited, 'Kameswarayya!' My name already known! And I had hardly met a single citizen of Nanjarajpet yet! I turned and found, to my consternation, Srikantayya. Though he was a man of Nanjarajpet, he had already met me on the road the previous evening. He had been repairing his cycle on the roadside but the moment he saw us he stopped us. He bullied our cartman and tied up his cycle on the roof, thrust himself into our midst, and reached the village. I understood him to be a mischievous and rowdy fellow. His call seemed to forebode some evil.

'To the Town Club, I suppose?' he asked.

'Yes, yes. I got the letter yesterday . . .'

'Come along! I am also going there.'

'I am glad I have met you. I want to get acquainted with all the big men of this new place.'

'Not many big men here, Headmaster. At least of the type you are after. The only man likely to engage a tutor is Mr Bhangarappa.'

'I saw him this morning . . .'

'Oh, so already you have been out hunting! The devil! What a nose you have for such things! Uncanny, I tell you. Was he in?'

'Yes; spoke to me very kindly; seems to be a very generous man.'

'Oh, stop that. He might have bamboozled you, Headmaster! Look here, don't talk of him in that style to anyone. We call him big only on the surface of our talk, but down below we call him a humbug, dastardly rascal. You haven't yet heard how his first wife died . . . unhappy woman! Starving for six months . . . But, why should that story come from me?

'Oh! How did it happen? Where?'

'Nothing happened. He is rich. He was an officer. And the evidence is not first-hand. No one actually saw him strangling her. It was at Tumkur that the lady died. But why should small men talk of big ones? Let it alone, Headmaster. Let us talk of your house. It is roomy enough? Houses here are brimful of scorpions. So keep your eyes open. Should the thing occur, send word to me. I know an effective magician.'

Just then three or four others joined us and Srikantayya introduced me to them. I was very happy to note that they were greatly pleased to meet the individual who was to preside over the education of their children . . . The only person who jarred on me was Srikantayya. The poison he poured into my ear gave me agony. How could I, after his insinuations, face Mr Bhangarappa, first thing every day? 'No' I thought. 'It could not be true. It must be the masterpiece of a local gossip. A deaf ear is all that it deserves.' I remembered how at Koppa I listened to the office peon of the Assistant Inspector of Schools. He had told me that the Saheb became slightly mad on every full moon

day and so when next the Inspector came to my
school and shouted at me on a full moon, I
attempted to tie on his wrist a protective
talisman, which I had purchased from the village
astrologer. It took me months of petitioning and
gallons of tears to get out of that mess. Once bit,
twice shy. So, I decided to allow all the prattle
of Nanjarajpet to enter one ear and leave by the
other.

The Town Hall was a little building set in a
wide compound, and consisted of a couple of
rooms and a hall. The building, rather proud of
its new brick-red coat, stood apart from its
surroundings, and bristled with flags and
festoons of mango leaves. The hall was already
half filled. Srikantayya got a special chair for
me and jammed it in an odd bit of space in the
fourth row. When he called out at the top of his
voice, 'Engta! Bring a big chair (the "big" was a
compliment to my girth) for the new
Headmaster!', everyone turned to look at me. If
only my turban, coat, and dhoti were a shade
cleaner, I should have been the proudest man at
that moment. And you too, my fellow teachers,
should be proud. For, when Srikantayya called out
those words, those memorable words, he was
honouring you and me . . .

The musicians had already spread themselves
out on the dais and were engaged in the
preliminary tasks of tuning up. Mr Bhangarappa
too arrived. He saw me and signalled from

where he was, 'How do you do?' I signalled back, 'Very well, thank you.' I then turned sharply round to discover how many persons had noticed this conversation.

Everyone seemed to be anxious for the programme to start, but it simply wouldn't. For, Sub-Registrar Mr Ram Singh, 'who in spite of his multifarious other engagements strove whole-heartedly to make this function a success and who had personally given a liberal donation of three rupees towards the cost of the portrait', had not arrived. The enlargement was prepared by no less a person than his own son-in-law, Mr B.R. Singh of Mysore. Therefore it was only in the fitness of things that we should all wait.

There was another cause too for the delay. The photograph of Mr Ramabhadrayya had not arrived. The four o'clock bus which was to have brought it was still on its way.

No wonder there was a great deal of coming and going, and peeping in and out by various functionaries of the club. Presently a servant sneaked in and gave a note to Mr Bhangarappa. It was, as we all expected, from the Sub-Registrar. He had a bad headache and so he proposed to leave home only after word was sent that the music was over. Hence Music *Vidwan* Naranappa had to start off with a certain unorthodox abruptness. His music provided a welcome background of noise for the indiscriminate chatter and loud speculations of the audience: What had happened to the bus? To whom did the carpet (spread on the floor for the occasion) belong? Was Mr Bhangarappa's moustache dyed or not? These were the problems that agitated those around me. Srikantayya and his group were busy investigating why Mr Ram Singh was keeping away. It couldn't be a headache, they clearly saw. Was there a flaw in courtesy when he was invited for the function? At last Srikantayya laid down his thesis: Ram Singh and Mr Bhangarappa had together gone the rounds in Mysore to select the photographer. They went into the son-in-law's studio. There, on the wall, the Inspector of Police saw a bromide enlargement of his first wife, prepared under orders from Mr Chinnappa (Mr Bhangarappa's son by his first wife). Mr Bhangarappa was very much shaken and he wanted to hurry out of the photographer's studio. But Mr Ram Singh insisted that he whould remain and give the order to B.R. Singh. That little rift widened day by day until you found the Sub-Registrar refusing to attend a function where the Inspector was the chief figure . . . I felt that the story was thin and patchy but kept my judgement severely to myself.

All of a sudden the music ceased, and everyone turned his eyes towards the dais. Goodness! What a scene! The drummer was lying prostrate beating the air with his hands, kicking, and frothing at the mouth, and with his eyes in a fixed stare. Some persons were fanning him, others dashing water on his brow, and someone was applying the good old remedy—forcing an iron key between the clenched teeth. The musician wailed, 'This monkey always falls down like this when I start singing. I knew this would happen. I had asked for another drummer. You people engaged this fellow because his services could be had free . . .' In this muddle, unnoticed, the violinist slipped out. As the crowd converged on the dais, Mr Bhangarappa recollected his police days and brandished his walking stick with good effect.

The confusion was so complete that no one noticed the arrival of the photograph ready for unveiling—tripod, green veil, and blue tape complete. I learnt that Srikantayya himself had taken charge of it as soon as the bus arrived for no one else in Nanjarajpet knew how to arrange the rings and tape in such a manner as to make a countenance slowly come to view, with a graceful tug. 'The business of preparing the portrait for the ceremony is mine. I don't need anybody's assistance,' Srikantayya is reported to have said, according to a friend of his, who added admiringly, 'And why would anyone go near the portrait now? We must be grateful to him for relieving us of all the bother. Who can understand all that rope and hook business? Moreover he is a terrible fellow. If he takes upon himself a task, he had better be left alone; if anyone interferes ever so slightly he would not hesitate to crack his skull . . .' Just then Srikantayya himself came and sat near us. After the drummer had been carried off to the veranda, Mr Bhangarappa got up to deliver his speech. The musician was still cursing the drummer. Srikantayya got up. 'I have to go now, Headmaster, for my *Sandhya* prayers,' he said and was off.

I did not catch much of Mr Bhangarappa's speech. His asthmatic voice could not penetrate the chatter around my chair. The following words kept coming up during the speech: 'Victoria Hospital . . . gout . . . Club . . . increment . . . Club . . . improvement eight years . . . Hassan Town . . . Pomegranate . . . Club . . . devotee of Shiva . . . Club . . . Nandikeswara . . . I.G. . . . I.G. Club . . . R.C. . . . God . . .' These were the only hints which helped me to reconstruct the career of Amildar Ramabhadrayya. When he said 'Club' the next time there was a vigorous clapping of hands, and it indicated the close of the peroration.

Mr Bhangarappa moved forward. He stepped on to the floor, proceeded with his own peculiar dignity towards the tripod near the wall. The secretary gave him the coloured tape and suggested that it might be pulled slightly to a side. Holding the loose end, Mr Bhangarappa stood for a moment facing the house. His face, one could see, was flushed with excitement. Then he said, 'May Mr Ramabhadrayya's smile scatter the sorrows of our daily toil. May God bless us that we may derive inspiration from this picture for many a year to come.' And then he gave the pull. The veil on the portrait fell away to a side.

A shriek! Mr Bhangarappa fell heavily into a chair beside him.

It was not Ramabhadrayya's portrait! . . . Some woman's instead! That woman's! Yes, Singh the photographer had sent to Nanjarajpet the enlargement ordered by Mr Chinnappa.

Was it all a conspiracy, I wondered, with Srikantayya as the arch conspirator? . . . Everyone was hilarious, shouting sarcasms, and yelling insults. They were pushing forward to see the photograph of the First Wife.

In that confusion no one attempted to help Mr Bhangarappa. I could not bear the injustice of it all. I pushed my way through the crowd to Mr Bhangarappa's chair. I applied a wet kerchief to his eyes and forehead. He rolled his eyes as if he had seen a fearful vision. He signed to me to take him out. I made him stand up and, resting on my arm, he moved to the veranda where a cool breeze was blowing. 'Oh! Is it you?' he whispered. 'Yes, I understand. The new Headmaster . . . the new man . . . you do not know. You have not yet heard their story,' he said. Then he walked a few steps. Leaning on my shoulder he swallowed a sob, and said, 'I lost her . . . Chinnappa's mother . . . God sent me this further sorrow . . . this horrible scandal and then this . . .'; he swooned in my arms.

Playlets

Watchman of the Lake

by
R.K. Narayan

INTRODUCTION

(On the eastern base of Baba Budan Hills, in Mysore State, there is an obscure little place now called Sakkrepatna, which at one time, a thousand or more years ago, was the capital of a king called Rukmangada. In the centre of this town there is a shrine which is dedicated not to distant gods or heroes but to a rustic, who was watchman of a lake called Ayyankere, four miles from the town. For purposes of this little drama, let us call him Mara, which is as good as any other handed down to us by tradition.)

SCENE ONE

(*A village at the foot of a hill. Road-menders at work.*)

Village Headman: Go on, boys, go on with your work. Hey, you, Racha, why do you stand looking at the sky? You there, you wretched dog, I will push you into the stream if I once again catch you gossiping with your neighbour. You dwarf, there, have you no better business than giggling and talking? The road must be ready before the king arrives. Just think for a moment, fools, how we should all look if the king suddenly came upon us! Just think: he will be here this time tomorrow . . . Go on, go on with your work, brother. Anyway what makes you all so merry? Let me know and share the joke. Come here, come here . . . (*commanding*) come here . . . why are you both laughing? Tell me, don't blink. What is it?

Two Timid Voices: Master, we are doing our work all right . . . But, but . . .

Headman: But what?

Timid Workmen: It is Mara.

Headman: Ah! Mara, what about him? Is that lunatic anywhere here?

A Timid Workman: Yes, yes, he was behind that rock and peeped at us. When you called he ran away.

Headman: Where is he now? Which way did he go?

Timid Workman: He sprang off like a buck and **ran up** the hill.

Headman: Here, stop all work. Put down your spades and crowbars; run and close round; stop all ways out; catch that thief and bring him here. Stun him with a blow if he resists. Bring him at once . . . Go . . .

(*The workmen throw down their implements and scatter about*)

(*They return, crying:* Master, here he is.)

Headman: Mara, you worthless dog! Have I not told you to keep away from here?

Mara: Yes, my master.

Headman: What do you mean by coming here and disturbing my workmen?

Mara: I am not disturbing them. I am here on my own work. Let them go on with theirs.

Headman: Don't talk of your work. Fool! You are a lunatic. Know it. Don't imagine you have any kind of work; the only work you have now is to disappear.

Mara: Why so?

Headman: Don't ask. I have told you the reason twenty times. The king is passing this way and I don't want him to know that our village has such fools as you.

Mara: I don't feel I am a fool.

Headman: Now listen. Keep out of our view the

next two days, when the king passes this way and back. Otherwise I will have you locked up in the cellar behind that old temple.

Mara: I will sit there and pray. If that God in the temple thinks I have work to do, he will take me out.

Headman: Now, get out of my presence. You fellows, why do you all stand gaping at me? Get on with your work . . .

Mara: Once again the Goddess of the river came to me in a dream and said: 'The king is coming this way. Tell him about the tank. He will listen.'

Headman: Don't tell me that again, you and your dream! I feel tempted to kick you.

Mara: What have I said to offend you so much, sir? Are you jealous that the Goddess comes to me rather than to you in dreams? Shall I repeat the very words she uttered?

Headman: No. Be off. And like a good fellow keep to your backyard till the king departs. I will give you a fine gift if you behave yourself.

Mara: Another person has already given me the greatest gift any man could give. Shall I say who that person is?

Headman: Oh! who is that great man?

Mara: My father-in-law.

(*The workmen laugh at this joke.*)

Headman: (*shouting in anger*) Stop laughing, everyone! I will starve you all without work if I catch you again laughing at this fellow's mad prattle. Shut up . . . Come here, Bhima. Throw down your crowbar. I have another piece of work for you. Come here.

Bhima: Yes, master, I have come. What is your command?

Headman: Bind this fellow hand and foot and throw him into the cellar behind the old temple, and keep him there till the day after tomorrow. Do you understand?

Bhima: Yes, master.

Headman: Mara, have a look at this giant. He can swing an elephant by its tail. So have a care. If you try any tricks on him, he will crush you out between his thumb and forefinger . . .

Mara: How did you manage to grow so fat?

Bhima: My mother gave me an iron decoction when I was a baby; and at every dawn I run up the hill with a large grindstone on my back. It is a very big stone. You can't move it even an inch.

Headman: Here, don't answer his questions.

Don't allow him to talk to you.

Mara: Why not? I too would like to grow fat and strong. If taking iron decoctions and carrying grindstones uphill could make me strong, why should I not try it? Maybe you will not think me mad then.

Bhima: You can't take the decoction now. Your mother should have put it into you before you were ten days old.

Headman: Bhima, don't you talk to him. Don't you see he is your prisoner?

Bhima: Yes, yes. I will be careful hereafter. But who will do my work here?

Headman: Don't concern yourself with it. You will get your wages all the same, perhaps a quarter more, if you do this bit of work well. Now take him away and sit over him till the evening of day after tomorrow. Take him away. Drag him like an animal if he gives trouble.

Mara: No, No. I won't give trouble. I will go with him gladly. Come on, come on. I will tell you all about my dream as we go.

Headman: Bhima, don't allow him to do that. He wants to talk to you and slip away while you are listening. Now bind up his wrists together with your turban and drag him behind you; gag him if possible . . . Ah, that is good, now it will keep him quiet. Now begone . . . How all our time has been wasted! Now swing your arms faster . . . You must have the path ready even if you have to work by lamplight after dark . . .

SCENE TWO

(*Trumpets blowing, restrained cheering of crowds, etc., announce the arrival of the king. Suddenly there is confusion. As the king is about to pass under a tree, someone jumps down from its branches.*

A *medley of voices crying:* Where did he jump from? Who is he? Hold him on . . .

King: Silence! Who is this man . . .?

Answering Voice: Your Gracious Majesty! This man . . .

King: We will hear the man himself speak.

Answering Voice: Your Majesty, he is unworthy of Your Majesty's notice.

King: We will hear the man himself speak. Let him be brought forward.
    (*The man is dragged before the king.*)

Who are you? Where did you drop from?

Mara: Your Gracious Majesty, I am an unworthy dog. But I have a word to convey to Your Gracious ears; and after I have uttered it, I shall gladly allow myself to be trampled under the feet of the mighty elephant which bears Your Royal Person.

King: Where were you all the time? On the tree?

Mara: Yes, Your Majesty. I was there since the cock crew this morning. I knew the Royal passage lay here.

King: Waiting on a tree! You could have asked for an audience.

Mara: They stoned me at sight; and commanded me to take myself out of the village; when I still appeared they tied me up and put me in a cellar, but the man who was my jailor, though a giant in appearance, has the soul of a baby. He let me go when he heard of my dream and the command of the Goddess. And I slipped out unseen and climbed this tree, and hid myself in its leaves, waiting and praying for Your Majesty's Gracious arrival.

King: What do you want?

Mara: Now listen to me, Most High. Where Your Majesty now stands is a sacred spot. There once stood the great Hanuman on the day Lakshmana was wounded in the battlefield at Lanka and lay in a deadly faint. Guided by omens Hanuman came here, and then he went up the mountain in whose shadow Your Majesty is resting now. There on its crest he found *Sanjeevini*. He flew

to Lanka with it, and at its breath Yama's
messengers fled, and Lakshmana rose to his
feet with a new life. Such was the power of
Sanjeevini; and where it grew there arose a
stream, which came down the mountain and
now flows past Your Majesty's feet. It is called
the Veda. Its water is the very lifeblood of Your
Majesty's humble subjects.

King: Do the waters flow in all the months of
the year?

Mara: Your Majesty, I am coming to it. The
water has flowed on since the day Hanuman
took the *Sanjeevini*. Its birth is in the fleeting
mists of the mountain-top, and it dances its way
through rare flowers and forests which clothe
the mountainside, before it comes down to our
village. And what do we do? My Lord, here I will
repeat the command of the Goddess: I saw her
in a vision as I lay in my hut. I had never seen
her before. She stood before me, her tresses
flying in the wind; there were stars in her
coronet; a ruby, as big as the eyes of that
elephant, sparkled on her forehead for a red
mark, her garment was of gold woven with
lightning. A look at her, and I knew it was the
Mother. I fell at her feet and she said: 'The river
Veda which you see at the foot of the hill and
from which you drink water, is my very own
plaything. It carries in its bosom the nectar
which revives gods and nourishes mortals . . .

But when the summer sun bakes your soil, I keep my pet sheltered in the cool glades of the mountain, and then you die of drought. When the sun goes and you have water, you take what you want and allow the precious stream to dissipate and perish in the foul marshes far off . . . I command you. Tell your king to build a bank and not to let Veda leave this village. Give her a home . . .' These were the words of the Goddess. I have repeated them. Your Majesty may trample me down under your elephant now.

King: Far from it. You have the grace of gods upon you. Your words are weighty . . . When we return this way tomorrow accompany us to the capital.

Mara: Forgive me Gracious One, I have only these rags to wear, and I am Mara the mad. How can I follow Your Majesty to the capital?

King: Our command is clear.

Mara: I obey.

SCENE THREE

(*Many years later. Mara is standing before his hut on the bank of a vast lake. There is a mingled noise of wavelets breaking upon the shore, cries of gulls, and the rustling of tree leaves.*)

Mara: (*Hallooing*) Boy, little man, Ganga, Ganga.

A Distant Voice: Father, I am coming.

Mara: Where are you gone, little man? (*Sound of running feet.*)

Ganga: Here I am, Father. You are shouting as if something or other had happened. I was only behind that tree watching . . .

Mara: What were you watching?

Ganga: There is a man fishing in the lake.

Mara: Fishing, fishing! Where? (*Runs. Son follows him.*)

Mara: Hey, man, get up! What are you doing here?

Man: Nothing.

Mara: Nothing! Then why that rod and hook in your hand? And how did all this fish come into your basket? Did they walk in while you were watching the sky? . . . Go, man, go before you are pushed into the lake.

Man: No. No, I was not catching fish. I speak the truth.

Mara: I have been a watchman of this lake for years and years, and I have come across hundreds of story-tellers like you. This is my last warning to you. If I see you again with that rod and hook, I will push you into the water; and the fish will feed on you. Do you understand?

Now here go your fish back where they belong.
Do you see my son? When I am gone you will be
the guard here; this is what you must do with
killers; whether they come with arrows for the
gulls which skim over the water, or with the rod
for the fish. This place is sacred and belongs to
the Goddess; and her command is that nothing
that flies or swims or walks in these parts
should ever be killed. From my hut I have often
seen at dead of night a tiger coming down from
the mountain and slaking its thirst at that
distant corner . . . But even that has to go
untouched; such is the command of the Goddess,
and the king's. Now begone, you fish . . .

Man: You are after all only a watchman. You
are not the master of this place. Are you not
taking upon yourself more than your duty?

Mara: I am the master of this place. The king
made me so. But for me Veda would have run
away and disappeared, as she was doing before.
It is I who gave her a home, where she stays,
and nourishes the corn fields of thousands of
the king's subjects . . . Now look along the bank;
do you note its length? A fling from the strongest
sling will not take a stone to the other end of the
bank; and I, by the king's order, watched every
stone with which this bank was built . . . and I
open the gates that let the water into the fields.
I know how much to give and when to stop, and
I tend the lake, and see that it is not polluted by

man or beast . . . Even that headman of the village who once beat and bullied me, will have to beg my permission if he wants to touch the water. Here I am the king; no one can question me. Now go away. I have spoken to you more than you deserve . . .

Now little fellow, my son, you see that man there taking his cow to the water's edge. Run on and tell him not to take it there; it is over a coconut-tree deep at that spot. If his cow slips . . . Tell him to move off a little. Go on, go on. (*The boy runs away.*)

A Visitor: Mara . . .

Mara: Oh, brother, when did you come?

Visitor: Just this moment. I left my village at sundown yesterday; and I have walked without a pause.

Mara: Come into my hut and have some food. There is bound to be something you can munch though nothing very good. My wife is away. I and my son are running the home.

Visitor: I have come all the way to ask a favour of you. You know our village is the farthest in our king's domain; and crops parch up and cattle are dying of drought. Will you give us some water?

Mara: Certainly, brother. It is here for all the king's subjects to take. Tomorrow I will come with you and see where you can lay the channels, and as soon as you have done it, the water is yours, it will be let to you according to the law laid down by the king. Ah, do you notice there the heart of the lake muddying! It was sapphire-like only a moment ago. Ah, see those clouds at the mountain-top . . . there is heavy rain there . . . Veda is swelling and carrying mud and flood into the lake. I must keep an eye on her tonight . . . (*calling*) Boy, come, come here, let us go in, I fear there will be heavy rain on us very soon.

SCENE FOUR

(*Late at night. Torrential downpour and a shrieking storm. The king's palace. The bell at the palace gate ringing incessantly.*)

King: Who is so urgently summoning me at this hour? What has happened in this terrible night of storm? Go down and see who it is.

(*The bell ceases, and sound of footsteps.*) Who are you, man? What has happened that you should be calling us at this hour? Why are you gasping so badly?

Man: I have been running.

King: In this storm? Who are you? What has happened?

Man: I am Mara, watchman of the lake, Most High.

King: Ah, Mara! How different you are now, battered by this rain, with your hair plastered on your face, and all that water dripping down!

Mara: I beg your Majesty's Grace for bringing my presence here in this state. I have come running, battling with roaring wind, and through slush and raging torrents . . . Forgive me, Your Majesty. I am trembling with the message within me. May I utter it?

King: Yes.

Mara: My Lord, it is the . . . it is about the lake . . . it is about the lake . . . I feel faint to mention it.

King: Oh, tell me, what has happened?

Mara: It is about to smash its bounds . . .

King: Mara, are you mad? Are you sure your mind is your own?

Mara: Your Majesty, till the evening there was no sign of a coming rain. It was a beautiful bright day; unruffled, the lake mirrored the blue sky on its bosom. But at dusk the sky darkened; I called my son in and shut the door of my hut. Raindrops battered my roof. At midnight the wind rocked my hut I got up and went out. My heart was disturbed.

King: Oh, tell me, is the lake going to break?

Mara: Your Majesty will know it presently. I

rose from my bed and went out. Ah, I have
never seen anything more terrible in my life, My
Lord. Veda was thundering down the mountain;
the wind shook the earth. I went to the edge of
the water; the waves rose to a man's height and
hammered at the bank; the water level was just
a hair's breadth below the shore. Any moment it
might heave and flow over.

King: Mara, Mara, was the lake, ah, what is to
happen to all of us?

Mara: I fell down and prayed. The Goddess
stood before me. Her tresses were wild, her eyes
gleamed with a strange light; she carried a
sword in her hand and she had splashed her
forehead with vermilion. I cowered at the sight
of her. 'Get up and hear me intently,' she said.
'I am the Goddess of the lake, and that river
Veda is my plaything. Clear out of your hut at
once.'

'Mother, save me. What is going to happen?' I
asked. 'I am going to kick away the miserable
stones you have piled up to imprison the waters
of my Veda. I am going to destroy your tank.'

'Mother, we put it up at your command,' I said.
'Yes, and now I want to destroy it. It is my mood
now. Veda is my plaything. I created it when I
wanted it, and I will splash away its waters
when I like. Who are you to stop me?' she
replied.

King: Mara, Mara, are you speaking the truth?

Mara: Your Majesty, may my son and wife perish if there is a word of untruth in what I am saying!

King: Go on with your story.

Mara: I pleaded with her. I pointed out to her the vastness of the lake, the water stretching the length of the hill and going in a bend out of sight; the whole of it kept back by a bank, which would take a quarter of a day to cross . . . But all that she would say to it was 'Why do you make much of it?' I told her that all that water waited like a crouching tiger and would spring upon the hundred villages and towns and the king's capital beyond, if the bank was removed. She laughed at it and flourished her sword. I pleaded with her for hours to spare us and have pity on us poor mortals. But she was not to be moved. A most terrible and reckless mood of destruction seemed to have come upon the Goddess. I fell on the wet ground, prostrated before her and begged: 'A poor mortal like me cannot stop you, oh, Divine Mother. But grant me this. I will run to the capital and inform the king, and return. Till then stay your hand. When you see me here again, you may carry out the devastation.' 'Yes, I grant this. I will wait until you have told the king and returned,' she said; and here I am, Your Majesty.

King: Mara, are you sure you saw and heard all this?

Mara: How can I prove it, My Lord? Here you see the mud on my clothes: When I fell prostrate before the Goddess, all this mud stuck to me.

King: I dare not think. I do not know what to do. In a moment or less I and this palace and my subjects . . . All right. Nothing so good as preparing for an end. Hey, call someone . . . Let an announcer go round with a beat of drums and announce to the people and to everyone in my kingdom that it is the last day of the world. The deluge is upon us. Tomorrow the sun will rise upon a lifeless land.

Mara: Your Majesty, permit me to . . .

King: Tell me, what have you to say?

Mara: I have a suggestion.

King: Go on.

Mara: The Goddess will keep her word. She has promised to wait till she sees me back there. Make it impossible for me to return there, Your Majesty.

King: How?

Mara: If Your Majesty's sword is there . . .

King: No, no. What a horrible suggestion!

Mara: Or send for the executioner, my Lord. My

son is still sleeping in the hut. My last request is this: when I am gone make him the watchman of the lake, and after him his son, and then his son's son to the last generation of our family.

SCENE FIVE

(*In front of a shrine on the lake. Ganga and his son.*)

Ganga: Son! Son! Come here.

Son: Coming father . . .

Ganga: Where were you all this time?

Son: I was watching the gulls flying over the lake, father. How they swim and catch fish! It is lovely to watch.

Ganga: Well, well, didn't you know this was the hour of worship at the shrine?

Son: Father, I forgot.

Ganga: Don't forget again, that is all I can say. I will be very angry if you miss another worship. You are old enough to realize your duties, I think. I was less than your age when I was ordered to take my father's place. Even my mother was away somewhere. The last I saw of my father was when I went to bed. When I woke up in the morning the hut had blown off, and the lake was nearly rolling over the shore. And whom should I see as soon as I got up but the king. He said my father was no more, and ordered me immediately to do my father's duties. Soon after that he built the shrine, which looks over the lake. And on the day of dedication he was himself present . . . You see those two figures, son. The one on the top pedestal is the Guardian Goddess of this lake. And the one immediately below it is my father. By the king's order worship is performed on the evenings of every Tuesday and Friday. Scores of people come from even distant town for it. You must not miss a single one henceforth.

Son: Yes, father.

Ganga: Good boy. When I am gone you must watch over this lake. After you, your son. Now come into the shrine and see the worship.

(*Ringing of temple bells.*)

The Blindman's Eye

by
N. Rajam

(*The Blindman's room in a house.*)
Blindman: Who is there?

Boy: Can't you see?

Blindman: How can I? I am blind, you know.

Boy: Oh, I forgot. I am your new boy. Your people have asked me to work from today. They have promised me ten rupees a month. You must increase it after six months.

Blindman: Certainly, if you are a good boy. What sort of a boy are you?

Boy: Of course, I am a good boy. Master (*lowering his voice*), I promise not to tell anyone, but tell me whether you are really blind or just pretending to be blind.

Blindman: I am honestly blind. I am not joking.

Boy: May I test you?

Blindman: Yes.

Boy: How many fingers do I hold up before you now?

Blindman: Two hundred. (*Laughs.*) Boy, now will you tell me something about yourself? Where did you work before you came here?

Boy: I was a ball-picker in a tennis court. Some days ago a ball was lost and they said I stole it and then drove me out.

Blindman: Did you steal the ball?

Boy: No, but I wish I had stolen it, master; in any case they call me a thief. There is a rascal in the second court who stole the ball. I will settle my score with him some day. They drove me out, and when I went home my father said he would send me to a school. Whenever I am out of work my father threatens to send me to a school. Is it fair?

Blindman: Why not go to a school?

Boy: Oh! You also think so! I went to a school for some time. I tremble even now to think of it. It is not a place for human beings. They beat and torture people there everyday. That is why I am always ready to do any work rather than go to a school. My father will be quiet as long as I am in some work. The moment I am out of one he will think of sending me to a school. If he is so fond of schools why didn't he go to one himself? This is what I don't like in elders. What is not good for them is good enough for us, I suppose?

Blindman: What is your name?

Boy: My name is Rama. But very few call me by my name. My father calls me Monkey; most of the people in the tennis court used to call me 'Hey' or 'Lazy Rascal'; and later they called me 'Thief'; and many people just call me 'Boy'.

Blindman: I will call you 'Rama'. It is a nice name. Vishnu, when he came down to the earth to destroy the ten-headed Ravana, was incarnated as Rama. It is a grand name.

Boy: You are very good not to call me 'Boy' or 'Rascal'. Will you tell me Rama's story someday? My father has often begun the story, but has never gone on with it. Something or other usually upsets him and he will break off and never take it up again for months and months.

Blindman: Perhaps he doesn't know the whole of the *Ramayana*.

Boy: Don't say so, master. He knows all our stories. The trouble is he is a very angry man and only very occasionally can we ask him for a story.

Blindman: If it is so, it will take over a hundred years for him to finish the *Ramayana* alone: and then there is the *Mahabharata* and numerous other things. Don't ask him for stories hereafter. I will tell you everything if I find that you are a good boy.

Boy: What should I do to be called good?

Blindman: You must be regular, punctual, and you must not trouble me. You must take me out every evening.

Boy: Where do you want to be taken?

Blindman: How can I say? You ought to know all the interesting places in the city. I will come with you anywhere. The previous boy was sent out because he wouldn't take me to any good place in spite of my repeated requests. Every evening he would take me to a stone bench in a nearby park, and I grew sick of it. He would seat me on the stone bench, slip away somewhere, and come back late in the evening and bring me back home. He was a very bad boy.

Boy: He was a bad boy, really. I won't do such a thing. I will take you to interesting places. You don't mind walking a little distance, do you?

Blindman: Not at all, I can walk for hours and hours.

Boy: Shall we go to a football match this evening, in that field near the tank? There is the final match between The Blues and The Muslims. It is going to be a thrilling match.

Blindman: We will go. Have we to buy tickets?

Boy: Yes, an anna per head.

Blindman: I will bring two annas.

Boy: Please don't waste the two annas, master; even if we get in you won't be able to see the match; as for me I can see the match without going in. Let us buy something to munch for two annas.

Blindman: How will you see the match without buying a ticket?

Boy: There is a tree outside. If we go there early we can get a seat on the branch; from there I can see the match very well. If you stay under the tree I will tell you everything that I see.

Blindman: You won't fall off?

Boy: Oh, no. I have seen hundreds of matches from that tree. Even if I have money I won't buy a ticket.

Blindman: I never knew the people did that sort of thing.

Boy: Tomorrow let us go to Nishat Bagh and hear the band; day after tomorrow let us go to the market. You will see how crowded it is in the evenings. On Sunday we will go to a lecture in the park near our house; but remember, you will have to tell me good stories all the way. If you don't, I will do as the previous boy did.

Blindman: Don't try to copy that bad boy. I will tell you long stories.

Boy: Master, another thing. Dasara is coming very soon. During those nine days you must let me go away after three o'clock everyday; only for nine days.

Blindman: Won't you take me along with you?

Boy: Impossible. I shall have to be running about and going to so many places everyday— palace, exhibition, tournaments, wrestling matches, and numerous other things. I can't take you because I shall be running from place to place.

Blindman: I am also eager to see the Dasara festivities.

Boy: Oh! Very well then. If you will let me go away at three o'clock everyday I will take you to the Maharaja's procession on the last day.

Blindman: I agree. You must keep your word.

Boy: I swear I will take you to the procession on the last day, but you mustn't keep me after three on other days or offer to come with me.

Blindman: Shall we go to a cinema some day?

Boy: No. You can't see and I won't see either, because I shall have to be telling you what is happening in the picture. It will be a waste of money. With that money we can by some good things to munch during our walks. No, never to a cinema.

SCENE TWO

Blindman: Is this the Clock Tower?

Boy: Yes.

Blindman: Do we go up?

Boy: Certainly not. They won't allow us there. We are at the foot of the Clock Tower. This is as far as we can go. We can see the procession very well from here. But cling fast to me; otherwise you will get lost.

Blindman: Yes, yes. Who is pressing on us?

Boy: I don't know. About twenty thousand fellows are pressing on us.

Blindman: Is it a big crowd?

Boy: Oh, yes. There is no room for all of them, and so most of the people are standing on only one leg.
(*The firing of a cannon is heard in the distance.*)
The procession has started from the palace. Hundreds of sepoys are coming. What gorgeous

dress they wear! Yellow trousers, green coats, and red turbans. I wish you had eyes!

Blindman: Is it the sound of their marching?

Boy: Of course it is. Here are some camels coming. They have two-hundred twists on their backs. Some fellows are sitting on them. It is a wonder that they don't fall off. I would not sit on a camel for anything. Here are some elephants. They are as dark and high as the Chamundi Hill. Hope they won't walk on us . . . Sirs, sirs, there is a blind man here. Don't push. Here are a thousand horses (*clatter of hoofs*), and what riders! They are carrying silver swords! I wish I could become a horseman too. (*Approaching sound of bugle and trumpets, and cheering of crowds.*)

Boy: (*Voice rising to a scream.*) Here is our Maharaja coming. Go on, clap your hands, master. Here is our Maharaja on his big elephant! What a howdah! It is made of diamonds and gold. The elephant has passed on . . . The crowd is breaking up, be careful, there is a lot of confusion. Ah, sirs, sirs, have pity on a blind man, don't try to trample him down; don't push, don't push; ah, master, let us go now. Come carefully, ah, where is my master? Who are you?

A Voice: Who are you?

Boy: Have I been holding your hand all the time?

Voice: I think so.

Boy: Where is my master? Oh, master, master, where are you?

Another Voice: Here, young fellow, why are you madly running about? Have you no eyes?

(*Sounding of various motor horns, and the noise of starting cars, and babble of crowd.*)

Boy: (*Crying.*) Did you see my master? Who has seen my master? (*A far-off cheering and clapping.*)

O, what shall I do now? Hundreds of cars will go about and knock my master down. (*Sobs and cries.*)

(*His cry,* 'Master! My blind master!' *is heard far and near, up and down above the babble of the crowd.*)

A Voice: What is the matter, little fellow, why are you crying?

Boy: I have lost my blind master; now hundreds and hundreds of cars will be going about and running over him, and thousands of people, what will they care for a blind man? They will trip him up from behind, walk on him, and crush him under their feet, and run their motor cars over him. Oh, oh, oh, . . . what shall I do? . . . oh, oh.

SCENE THREE

(It is midnight. Blindman's room in the house.)

Boy: I have come to announce that my blind master has been lost in the procession crowd. He is probably dead now. I couldn't find him though I have gone round and round the whole city and can't walk anymore.

Sleeper: Who is there? Rama!

Boy: *(In ecstasy.)* Master, are you the person lying on the bench?

Blindman: Yes.

Boy: Master, are you sure?

Blindman: Rama, Rama, where are you?

Boy: I am outside your window, master. I am holding on to the bars.

Blindman: You are a bad boy. Why did you leave me in the crowd and go away?

Boy: Don't call me a bad boy, master. Goddess Chamundi knows that I am not lying. I didn't know that I was holding someone else's hand in the crowd. How did you come back, master?

Blindman: I didn't know that I had my hands on someone else's shoulder. At any rate I think I had my hands on your shoulder when you said

that the Maharaja's elephant was passing us, but immediately after that I was rushed, knocked down and so on. I thought my end had come when I realized that you were not there. But some good people protected me and brought me home. I don't know who they are. And what do you think I have done today? I walked from the gate into the house all by myself.
(*Sobbing noise from the boy.*)

Blindman: Rama, are you crying?

Boy: Yes. Your people will dismiss me in the morning, and then my father will send me to a school.

Blindman: Don't cry. Now listen (*lowering his voice*), I don't think there was anyone in the hall when I came in, and no one knows, and I won't tell anyone.

Rama: Will you swear that you won't?

Blindman: Certainly.

Rama: You are a god, you are a saint, my master. You are a very good man. I will take you to a cinema tomorrow, if you will give me money for the tickets. I promise I will. I will now go home, eat, and sleep; I am tired; I have wandered all over the city today. You are a god, master. Lie down and sleep. I will come early in the morning.

Blindman: Are you holding on to the window bars?

Boy: Yes, master.

Blindman: Jump down carefully and go home. (*Rama jumps down and runs away.*)

Translations

Lyric Pearls from Sanskrit

by
T.N. Sreekantaiya

A cultured Indian, even he is unfamiliar with
Sanskrit, will have read in some translation
plays like the *Sakuntala* and the *Mrcchakatika*—
plays which have become a part of the world's
heritage. He will have heard of a heroic peom
like the *Raghuvamsa* and a prose romance like
the *Kadambari*, and is likely to have an idea of
their contents. He is sure to know that Sanskrit
abounds in epigrams which distil in a couple of
lines the essence of a lifetime's observation and
meditation; when the occasion provokes he may
even be able to quote a few bits of them. But
what about the lyric, perhaps the purest form of
poetry? Have we in Sanskrit this brief but intense
expression of human emotion in its myriad

moods—now light, now serious; now bitter, now
serene; now sparkling like a gem, now profound
as the sea; simple in structure, undeflected in
its course, and, in a few selected words,
illumining a dark corner of the human heart or
revealing a whole aspect of human life? There is
in Sanskrit a type of lyric which rises to the
highest levels of poetry; but the ordinary reader
is not to blame if he is hardly aware of its
existence. These poems are mostly found in
bulky ancient anthologies like the
Suktimuktavali, the *Saduktikarnamrta*, the
Subhasitavali, etc., guarded by learned
instroductions. Brief accounts of them may
appear in histories of Sanskrit literature, but
the ordinary reader fights shy of these rather
forbidding volumes. Articles primarily devoted
to an exposition of the beauty of these poems
are quite a rarity; and even these, barring a few
exceptions, rest between the covers of some
research journal. No wonder that these lyric
treasures remain all but inaccessible to the
uninitiated.

I have here selected from diverse sources just
a handful of these masterpieces for presentation
in an English garb. A metrical rendering was
out of the question. The haunting music of the
original Sanskrit, its subtle alliterations and
assonances, its suggestive word order, the lilt of
its metres: I have not aspired to reproduce these
untranslatable excellences. In the prose version

that follows, which I hope is neither too literal nor too free, I shall feel happy if I have succeeded in conveying at least the thought-content of the original pieces. Great poetry, it is said, breaks through the barriers of language and survives even the ravages of translation. It is this faith which has emboldened me to render these masterpieces into a foreign tongue.

A few words of introduction are necessary. An obvious feature of these poems is their extreme shortness. Each stanza, consisting of only four lines, is a complete poem in itself. It is like an exquisite miniature painting done on a two-inch bit of ivory. It contains all that a responsive reader needs for full appreciation. He has only to keep his imagination awake and allow it to hover around the poem.

The limitations imposed by the narrow span of a single stanza are indeed rigorous. The poet cannot stretch a description or elaborate a point; he can hardly waste a word. He must choose only the most significant situations and details, and even these he must rather suggest than express in so many words. The Sanskrit poet accepts this challenge. The poems given here can bear ample testimony to his victory.

In Sanskrit, such pieces go by the general name *muktaka*, meaning 'that which is free or detached'. A large majority of them must have been composed as independent lyrics, as the mood or occasion inspired the poet. No doubt some of them, found in the anthologies, originally formed part of a longer poem; but now they shine by their own light, independent of the context. Thus both these kinds fully deserve the name *muktaka*. We may also note that in the term *muktaka* there is an appropriate as well as obvious suggestion of *mukta*, 'a pearl'.

The range of these 'lyric pearls' is as wide as life itself. Among the numberless themes, however, love is the particular favourite of the poets. And what an astonishing variety and richness do we find in their portrayal of this old, old subject! From the first dawn of this disturbing emotion to the final union or bereavement, through the whole gamut of admiration, longing, hope, despondency, meeting, discord, separation, jealousy, remorse, reconciliation and so on— there is no phase of love that the Sanskrit poet cannot depict with feeling, insight and delicacy. Many of these love lyrics are as fresh today as they were centuries ago when they appeared in their first bloom. Some of the loveliest of them are to be found in the *Amarusataka*, a century of verses attributed to the poet Amaru (or Amaruka). As an old saying indicates, a stanza of Amaruka is worth a hundred elaborate poems.

Then we have the unique *anyokti*, 'veiled utterance'. In this type, the poet ostensibly sets out to describe or apostrophize a natural object like some tree or animal, the sea or the desert, even the sun or the moon—in fact, everything in the Universe, outside man. The poet's statements no doubt fittingly apply to the chosen subject; but it is obvious to the discerning reader that he is aiming at something beyond. It is really some human trait that he is depicting, some human misery that he is bewailing, some human folly that he is satirizing and some human institution that he is attacking. The effect of such a poem is all the greater since there is no direct reference anywhere in it to the poet's ultimate intention.

Now to a contemplation of the little masterpieces themselves. We shall of course begin with love. Here is a person who has discovered that the state of love is an unbearable agony:

Mere thought of her throws me into fever; the very sight of her drives me mad; and at her touch I fall into a swoon. How can she be my tender one?

Can a person deep in love ever know happy moments? A woman tenderly reproaches her lover:

When you are not before me I long to see you! When you are with me I fear I shall lose you. Neither in your absence nor in your presence have I any joy.

The utter poignancy of separation has never perhaps been better measured than in this contrast:

*Not even a necklace did we wear for fear it
would part us in our embrace. Now there
spread between us hills, rivers and woods.*

Some of these lyrics are in the form of a
dialogue. This is how an *abhisarika*, a woman
going out on love's quest, answers an interlocutor:

*'Whither are you bound, fair lady, in the
thick of the night?' 'Thither where lives my
lover, the lord of my life.' 'You are alone; tell
me, girl, if you are not afraid.' 'But, have I
not at my side Cupid with the feathered
arrows?'*

Quarrels are an inevitable part of love life.
To judge from the poetic material before us, the
offender in those classical times was usually the
male. His lady love, however, would not bear it
all meekly; she had her own ways of punishing
him. *Manini*, 'the offended woman', is a constant
theme of these lyrics. If the culprit had any
spark of love left in him, nothing could be more
effective than this unusual but supreme
punishment:

*She did not bar the door against him, did
not turn away from him, did not even utter
hot words of anger. Only, with unfaltering
eyes she looked at her lover as at any one else!*

Here is another *manini*. She is pointing to
her lover the depth of degradation to which

their love has sunk. Alas, she finds cause to be as bitter against herself as against her lover:

Where the height of anger was confined to a frown, the sole punishment was silence, a mutual smile meant conciliation and a full glance was gracious favour;—see what a disaster has befallen that love of ours! You lie at my feet, writhing; and yet, anger has not left my wretched self.

In the next piece, the tragedy is complete and the disillusioned victim bewails:

'This is black.' 'Black it is.' 'But, dearest, surely it is white!' 'What else can it be?' 'We shall now go out.' 'Yes, we shall.' 'Enough of walking.' 'Be it so.'—The very person who thus studied every whim of mine in the past has now become a stranger. Oh friend, who can ever know men?

Before taking leave of this theme, let us quote a stanza which reveals in a flash the secret of love's magic:

My beloved does only what pleases me: thus he thinks, but knows not that whatever she does pleases him.

From passion to renunciation seems a far cry. But a devotee of the senses will himself admit the profound truth of the following observation; it is a poet and not a barren moralist that is speaking here:

It is true, women are charming: it is true, riches are alluring. But verily, life itself is fickle like the wink of a drunken wench.

There can be grim harmony in the very citadel of ruin; but one requires an artist's eye as well as a philosopher's soul to appreciate it. Here is one such spirit:

This village deserted, this temple in ruins, this pond in front dried up, this tree here with withered branches; and I myself, a wanderer with my fortune all run out: this meeting of equals, though bitter, amuses me.

We shall turn again to the workaday world. Here is a simple, straightforward description of a not uncommon situation. But how vivid the details are, and how sad is their appeal to the sympathetic heart:

He opens his eyes wide, rubs them close with his hand, now moves the thing to a distance, now draws it very near, goes out into the sun and remembers with regret the past excellence of his eyesight. Thus he behaves, on the threshold of old age, with a book before him.

We now come to the *anyokti* group. The following one is addressed to an ungrateful elephant. Neither in this piece nor in the others

selected here is there any necessity to interpret
for the reader the obvious human significance of
the 'veiled utterance':

> *Here you have drunk ice-cool water, eaten*
> *lotus-sprouts, and bathed and refreshed your*
> *limbs when the heat was oppressive. Fie on*
> *you, oh elephant-prince, that you should now*
> *foul the waters of the very lake, trample on its*
> *lotus-stalks, and uproot its banks! Does not*
> *even shame bestir in you?*

The next poem also concerns an elephant,
but how different the situation! It is the story of
a simple-hearted elephant's rush into captivity,
with the distressing but inevitable conclusion.
The logic of the events is so relentless that the
reader has to bear it in mute anguish. The poet
has deepened the pathos by making the elephant
himself the speaker:

> *I left Mount Vindhya that was a father to*
> *me, the divine river Narmada so like a*
> *mother, and those dearly attached elephants,*
> *my companions since birth. Lured by my*
> *passion for you, oh elephant maid, myself did*
> *I lead this body to bondage. Now you are kept*
> *away from me while stinging goads score my*
> *forehead.*

There is devastating satire in the following
advice to the washerman's ass, proverbial for its
stupid and miserable existence:

> *Oh ass, why do you carry heavy loads of*
> *clothes and munch some detestable stuff? Go*
> *to the royal stables and dine at your ease on*
> *gram-gruel! All that wears a tail is a horse to*
> *the officers there in authority. The king*
> *believes whatever they report. And all the rest*
> *observe strict unconcern.*

As a final example, we may give this brilliant little piece in which the gnarled and thorny *khadira* tree is seemingly made the target of attack:

> *We tolerate serpents in the sandalwood*
> *tree. For, how can a thing of beauty remain*
> *unguarded? But tell us, oh khadira tree, to*
> *guard what excellence of thine hast thou*
> *gathered these thorns?*

Some idea of the charm and variety of the Sanskrit *muktaka* must have been gathered by the reader even from the few examples presented here. The poets themselves were fully alive to its sweetness. In the following witty lines, one of them proves the superiority of the *subhasita* over the sweetest things we know of by skilfully presenting their normal condition itself as an evidence of their discomfiture. The term *subhasita* (or *sukti*), we may note in passing, means 'a fine saying'; it includes our lyrical *muktaka*:

The grape wears a withered look, sugar has turned into stone; afraid of facing the sweet subhasita, ambrosia itself has fled to heaven!

The Thief's Songs

by
K. Chandrasekharan

In Sanskrit literature, besides the celebrated names of the first rank, there are many poets and writers whose memory will last as long as fancy and feeling inspire our hearts. Bilhana is such a one. He lived in the 11th century AD. His *Choura-Panchasika*, meaning *The Fifty Verses of the Thief* would at once provoke curiosity as to why such a name should have been given to a poet's song. Indeed, there is as much charm in the lines ascribed to him as in the story encircling his name.

Tradition says that there was a king named Madanabhirama, who ruled over the Panchalas, having as his capital a city called Lakshmimandiram. His beautiful daughter, Yamini Poorna Tilaka (the Full Moon of the Night) was young and learned in all the arts except literature. Her father naturally desired her to be versed in literature also. So, from a number of applicants to the post of a tutor for his daughter, he selected Bilhana, the poet. Bilhana was exceedingly handsome, and unequalled in literary equipment. The worldly-wise minister of the king shrewdly guessed the danger of engaging such an attractive young man to teach one who was lovely and just of the age to be attracted by youth and good looks. He knew that the princess abhorred to see blindness and also knew that Bilhana hated to see lepers. So he informed the princess that her tutor was blind and Bilhana that the princess was suffering from the incurable disease which he loathed to see. A thick curtain was therefore hung in the chamber, on either side of which were seated the tutor and the taught, the one pouring out his lore and the other listening to the magic of his words.

Days rolled on thus. On an evening before the rise of the full moon, Bilhana strayed into the queen's garden, where the princess was also present, all alone. Without being aware of the royal presence, he burst into poetry, praising the full moon. The princess heard the familiar voice and rushing to the spot found Bilhana, handsome and blessed with eyesight. Bilhana too came to know who she was and was struck with her beauty. The trick played upon them by the king's minister became clear to them both.

Love's arrow was quick in its work, and soon both preceptor and pupil found themselves lost in each other's company. When the king came to know of their secret love, he condemned the poet, the stealer of his daughter's heart, to the scaffold. As Bilhana reached the execution spot, the executioners were much intrigued to find a smile playing upon their victim's lips. Questioned as to this strange behaviour, he replied to them that he was happy because of the memory of his sweetheart. So saying he began to compose lines and thus fifty verses coursed down his lips. Marvelling at such a flow of poetry from his lips, the executioners ran to the king to report the matter. The king came to the spot himself and found the poet still in a sweet trance with his lips uttering the name of the deity of his heart, his own daughter. The king was convinced of Bilhana's true love. Yamini Poorna Tilaka was thereafter given away in marriage to the poet.

Now to the verses themselves, which, though not profound in poetic conceit, are enchantingly simple and descriptive. The purport of a few of them is given here in prose translation; for it is an impossible task to capture the form and spirit of the Sanskrit lines.

* * *

Even now I dwell upon her alone, whose soft skin bears the whitish-yellow of the champaka bloom, whose eyes are like the petals of the full-

blossomed lotus . . . Awakened from her sleep and weary of love's fatiguing intoxication, she tries to elude me even as knowledge slips away by long neglect.

* * *

Even now let my mind fondly trace my sweetheart's face, which is white and rosy as the inside of the full blown lotus, with the mark of sweet-scented Gorochana on her forehead and her glances rolling slightly with love's wine.

* * *

Even now my heart is fixed on her. In the night I sneezed* she would refuse petulantly to utter the usual prayer, 'May you live long', but saying nothing would place on my ears the flowers of gold.

* * *

Even now I do not forget her fine set of teeth resembling the kunda buds, and her mischievous glances stealing from the edges of her eyes. Can I help remembering her beautiful face! Can gratitude help remembering good deeds done!

* * *

---

*It is usual custom for a person when he hears a child sneeze, to say 'May you live long!' The belief is that a prayer at such a moment will ensure the child long life. Here, in this verse, there is a hint that the lover adapts an old custom to serve his own needs: when he is troubled by his beloved's silence, he resorts to sneezing in the hope that it will compel her to speak.

Even now I recollect her getting impatient and angry with me, while copious tears choked her words with indignation rising in her throat and deep sighs parching up her lips.

* * *

Even now I feel I see her looking in secrecy into the mirror and getting disturbed on finding me in the reflection behind her; her heart will be then agitated, her body heave in confusion and shyness overcome her, because of love's presence.

* * *

Even now I remember her. listlessly roaming about, to and fro, inside and out, all because of my absence. I can picture her golden-lotus face turning charmingly away followed by her glances.

* * *

Even now I remember her turning on her side in bed, in spite of my attempt to please her; her pretensions to be alseep in my presence; but with the morning, her hand lying on me.

* * *

Even now I remember her getting thrilled all over with intense expectation at my sight, though, when asked by her girl-friends 'Who is he?', she of the dreamy eyes, will open them wide in surprise and reply 'Not that I know of.'

* * *

Even now I feel her concealed like a bee in the petals of my heart. May the Fates mercifully decree that in my next birth at least I shall be happy with her and never be separated from the fawn-eyed girl of my heart, who is more charming in her love.

* * *

Even now ye executioners stand by your duty, just as God Siva will not give up his Kalakuta poison, even as Mahavishnu *in his Kurma Avataram will not give up the burden of the earth on his back, and even as the mighty ocean will not cease to keep the unbearable fire* within its bosom!*

---

*The mythological fire called *Badavanala*.

Glimpses of Tamil Poetry

(War and Peace)

by
Madukaran

The most delectable aspects of love reveal
themselves only in a mock quarrel, which will
suddenly afflict the lovers. (It is called *Oodal* in
Tamil). At a moment of intense companionship
a sudden anger will come upon the lady. She
will cry 'Come not near me!', wrench her hand
free, and display utter hostility. On examination
no cause can be found. She will have imagined
a wrong and taken offence. It is now her lover's
great duty to soothen her temper and regain her
favour. A woman in such a state will not listen
to much argument—a fact well realized by the
lover. So he will do the best thing under the

circumstance: he will fall at her feet crying, 'I am vanquished!' On hearing it, she will naturally soften; and he will drive home, very gently and gradually of course, the fact that he did not merit her anger. Even after her anger has left, she will still hold herself aloof, unable to know how to become friendly all of a sudden. How long? Till she finds the flimsiest excuse. Just as she suddenly invented an excuse for declaring war, she can also discover an excuse to announce peace. Our poets have very elegantly dealt with this subject—the coming of anger and its going. An incident of this kind I shall take from a work called *Jeevaka Chintamani* written a thousand years ago by Tiruthakka Devar.

(The following is a broad paraphase of a few stanzas rather than a translation.)

The hero of *Jeevaka Chintamani* is Jeevakan, a prince who after distinguishing himself in various battles, returned to his capital and married a princess called Elakkanai. They were in their chamber. Sweet incense filled the air. Flower-garlanded Jeevakan and Elakkanai rested on their silken couch, little knowing whether it was they or their feelings which met in the ecstasy of companionship. At that moment he fixed his eyes on Elakkanai's face. Her beauty held him in such a spell that he gazed fixedly, without winking his eyelids. This made his eyes smart and water. Elakkanai noticed it and thought, 'Here is this man shedding tears at the memory of someone else,' and cried aloud, 'What is this! It is folly to be in the caress of one who weeps thinking of someone else.' She was overcome with grief and anger. Her sharp eyes spat fire. She rubbed out the sandal paste smeared on her arm; tore off her flower-garland; cracked her little fingers which were adorned with rings; sobbed; looked him up and down; and stood off, her lotus-like face beaded with perspiration. What could he do in this emergency? He was distressed. He did not venture to explain. He cried, 'Ah, my life is gone!' and held her pink-tinted, jewel-sparkling, tiny feet. His abject despair touched her heart. A little tenderness returned to her eyes. Jeevakan realized that grace was coming and said, 'You tender one, graceful as a flower-creeper, you who adds brilliance to the brilliants which adorn you; it was by gazing on you that my eyes watered. Can you not bear this mishap for a while?' But she still appeared to be unmoved. He cried, 'The sins of my previous births are great and have brought on me this suffering . . . Oh, honey-bees caress this lady with your wings and tell her to give me the boon of her grace.'

This appeal was heard by a parrot and a mynah which were in a cage. They put their beaks through the bars, peeped down, and remarked to each other. 'The beloved one of our king's—is her heart of stone or iron? When we are in a similar mood, if our men appeal to us so desperately, we will collapse, not having the strength to bear the sight of their humiliation.' They cried to Elakkanai, 'Oh, lady, he has committed no wrong. We beg of you, have a heart and do not torment him.' Following this, another bird was suddenly seized with a doubt and said to the parrot, 'You fool, our lot is to live in this cage and feed on what is thrown to us. If you presume to advise, this gold-bangled fair one will not show us a morsel of food for three days. So, you good parrot, take my warning and shut up.' This was a bird who weighed causes and effects and calculated. But the parrot was one who had consideration for justice alone, and was not concerned with its own security and food, and so it cast all caution to the winds and said, 'Even if he has committed a grievous wrong, if he touches her feet, a woman must show grace. That is the mark of a woman of true breeding. A woman who is heartless as the one here makes even gold-snatching, public women look virtuous by comparison. Even if I am the mother who has begotten this lady, I cannot bear to see the cruelty she is inflicting, and live. Hence I will hang myself.' So saying the parrot twisted a cord which was dangling inside the cage around its neck.

Elakkanai saw this and was stunned for a moment; and then she burst out laughing. Laughter is a universal solvent. Jeevakan cried, 'Oh, bird, may you be blessed with long life! I have attained the boon I wanted, through your kindness,' and embraced his beloved and praised her beauty. She listened to him for a long while, and being unable to maintain her gravity any longer, said, 'Don't try to captivate me by singing my praise. I know what I am. A person who has for pets creatures of low breeding such as these birds—what utter depravity can she not sink to?' She said this and offered to her husband the nectar of a laughing face at which they forgot their quarrel and lived in a joy which was now ten times greater.

* * *

Since His Sceptre is Straight

by
Kapilar

(Translated from Tamil by P.N. Appuswami)
NOTE: Kapila the poet praises his patron's hill, lamenting his death.

Saturn, the dark planet, may smoulder,
Or the earth be enveloped in smoke,
Or Venus fly southwards;
Yet crops teem in the fields;
And flowers blossom on the shrubs;
And large herds of tender-eyed kine,
Which have calved in the homestead,
Browse at ease on the fair grass;

Since his sceptre is straight,
The wise throng there;
And his fields have never known the rains to
    fail;
There the green-leaved jasmine buds white
Like the sharp teeth of a kitten.
Such is the country ruled by the father
Of these choice-bangled maidens.

* * *

Fragrant Tresses

by
Irayanar·

(Translated from Tamil by P.N. Appuswami)

NOTE: A king addresses a bee hovering round his lady's
tresses. He asks it a question and bids it answer fair.

O Honey-bee with beauteous wings
Whose very life is a quest of flowers!
I charge thee speak—but impartial be,
And tell me truly what you know.
Is there a flower of all your flowers
Which has the fragrance of her tresses,
My love, my own,
With peacock grace,
And perfect teeth?

* * *

My Heart is Aching

by
Kamam-Ser-Kulattar

(Translated from Tamil by P.N. Appuswami)

NOTE: The lady comforts her maid who deplores the forlorn state of her mistress.

My heart is aching, aching;
And my eyelids hold back the scalding tears;
Since he who sat by my side
And soothed and comforted me
Is now parted from me
And is himself disconsolate, comfortless.
For him
My heart is aching, aching.

* * *

The Cruel Lover

by
Mutu-Kurranar

(Translated from Tamil by P.N. Appuswami)

Almost reverently, as if in adoration,
He placed my hands upon his eyes;
And with his hands stroked my fair forehead;
And mother-like spoke sweet words to me;

But cruel as a robber is he, alas! alas!
He the lord of those high-crested hills,
Where falling cascades glisten like gems,
And scattered *vengai* flowers gleam
Like gold upon the slopes;
While on the peaks
The waving bamboo—tall, green-jointed
Rips the rain-clouds as they flee.
Ah! Cruel alas is he!

('My Heart is Aching' and 'Fragrant Tresses' are
from *Kuruntokai*. 'Since His Sceptre is Straight'
is from *Purananooru*. 'The Cruel Lover' is from
Narrinai. These poems are about two hundred
years old.)

Studies

Good Earth

by
N.R.

Something of romantic interest has always belonged to the cultivation of land, especially in the minds of people who, in the turmoil of urban occupations, have found solace in the contemplation of a life close to nature. The weary merchant or lawyer or public servant pictures it to himself as a life of carefree communion touched with the glamour of sunrise and sunset, and the changing seasons. There is poetry in the very name of the Earth—*Sarvam Saha*—the all-enduring mother, who nourishes all, and in the end gathers all, like tired children, to her bosom. When we reflect how large a proportion of our people live by agriculture without audible discontent, we are apt to conclude that land never betrays trust, but always yields a living to those who seek it of her. So we love to think, and so it should be, in an ideal world of perfect adjustments.

Though long years of work as a revenue officer had dimmed the first brightness of my faith in agriculture, I considered that with wisdom and management there was a living to be made out of land, and that village life might provide a welcome occasional change from the routine of other occupations. I also thought that when in the usual course, the time came for retiring from strenuous service agriculture in a quiet faraway village, it would be a life of peace with just the right admixture of unexacting work, a life in which the hours would glide lightly between work in the open air, good books, and kindly relations with neighbours.

That was what I promised to myself when I became owner of an estate in a promising tract recently brought under irrigation by a river channel. I have now spent some of the precious evening years of my life in trying out the plan I made. I have put money and work in it, and all things considered I have not done badly. I have seen the seasons come and go, and the sun and the rain ripen the corn. I have seen the many-sided sorrow and gladness of village life; I have made many friends, and I hope not any enemies. I love the life with which I have lived, its simple joys, its many sorrows—the hunger, the pain, and the disease, borne with patient faith and heroism. I have seen appalling poverty and ignorance. I have seen children die for want of help and food; I have seen much avoidable suffering and death. I have wondered that such things should be in our times and midst, and tried to understand the root of the evil. That the Earth is kind is poetry, but that nature is cruel—as cruel as beautiful—is an unfortunate fact. A great physician—I cannot recall the name—once said to a good-natured optimist: 'Leave the cure to nature? Why, my dear sir, nature has no use for the sick man. She would soon see him in his grave!' The cultivator is left largely to the care of nature, with insufficient equipment and subject to the heavy handicap of an antiquated and inequitable land revenue system.

'Antiquated land revenue system'—what do I mean by that? Do I, forgetting that I am a superannuated man myself, foolishly hint that a thing is bad merely because it is old? By no means; I wish to point out that a thing originally good may, in a changing world, have out-lasted its usefulness. That is what has happened with our land revenue system, derived from a traditional polity in which the King was the owner of all the soil, and was entitled to take a sixth of the gross produce. But in that same polity the King was directly responsible for the health and happiness of every subject however poor or humble:

'From imparting culture to his subjects
and from protecting and supporting them,
he was verily their father; the parents
who begot them were merely physical
causes.'

That is to say, the education, and physical
welfare of every subject was the immediate
concern of the King. He guaranteed to all his
subjects the requisites of a happy physical and
mental life. This immediacy was possible—was
conceivable—only in a small state, not far
removed from the family and the tribe from
which it had evolved. It was possible only in
States so small, and under conditions so intimate,
that men could break into the royal presence
shouting '*Abrahmanyam* (Outrage!)' and dump
corpses of their untimely dead at the door of the
King in proof that something was rotten in the
State. How it worked in practice, we do not
know; great and good Kings like those of Manu's
race must have been exceptions, for it is the
exception that is apotheosized, and not the rule.

Few will contend that the ideal of duty
towards the subjects is, or should be, less high
in the modern State. If, in such a State, we find
in operation a levy which cuts even into the
minimum of a bare animal life, it should give us
furiously to think. The land revenue as assessed
and levied in Mysore in common with the rest of
India, is such an imposition.

No State can avoid taxation, but justifiable taxes are derived from surplus, and not snatched out of the very necessaries of life. Wise taxation should not impair the means of production. There can be no doubt that the land revenue, which cleaves like *karma* to every holding however small, is neither justifiable nor wise in the case of small holdings of peasant proprietors. With hard work and fair seasons an average cultivator's family of five can just live at the low standard which makes no allowance for savings or leisure, on an estate of about ten acres of dry, or its equivalent of irrigated land. The area may be put a little higher, or a little lower, according to personal predilections and the nature of the soil—but this does not affect the validity of the argument. At this level the family maintains itself in the physical fitness necessary for agricultural work—that is to say, the members are efficient human livestock. There is no surplus out of which any tax could be paid; and if a tax has to be paid, it has to be cut out of the food, or the clothing, or the conventional necessaries of the family. It is no use to say that some of these conventional necessaries, such as expenditure on feasts, weddings, etc., should be retrenched; the fact remains that the peasant would rather cut his food than them; in other words they *are* necessaries.

Now if the land revenue is a deduction from the necessaries of life, it certainly affects the cultivator's health and strength, and his efficiency as a factor of production. Leaving aside human values for the moment, he becomes less economical as farmstock.

When the peasant has not the wherewithal for keeping himself and his family in good physical shape, what need to say that he is utterly unable to improve his land or industrialize his cultivation? The land tax that is taken from a cultivator whose estate is so small that it yields no surplus over the scanty rations of the family which works it, impairs the two essential factors of production—the *man* and the *land*—and yet both these are the very life of the State.

When it is seen that a very large portion of the holdings in Mysore are of less than the area which can yield a bare living, some idea may be formed of the magnitude of the evil done by the system in which no estate—that is to say, no agricultural return—however small is exempt from taxation. An argument sometimes heard is that the cultivator has subsidiary sources of income as a coolie but this only makes the case worse, for it means that his life is regarded as a taxable commodity. What wonder that agricultural indebtedness is steadily growing? What wonder that the tax-collector coming round at harvest time, converts that time of gladness into one of tribulation, and that the land is but languidly worked by people who get so little out of it?

In the case of the income-tax, which falls on an economically higher taxable capacity, a minimum is recognized below which taxation is not justifiable; but the agriculturist is considered fair game, however feeble, and finds no mercy. And yet agriculturists are the bulk of the population, and practise the one industry without which no other industry would be possible.

Is there no help for this state of things? Several obvious courses present themselves. Increasing the cultivator's return from land by improving and financing agriculture, starting subsidiary industries, preventing fragmentation of holdings, consolidation of holdings—these are all remedies so far as they result in giving the cultivator a taxable surplus. But they take time and patience, and far-sighted planning and investment. And besides, present generations should not left to their fate, to toil without joy or hope. Let us show 'the heavens more just'.

What *can* be done is a redistribution of the burden of taxation. This is no insoluble problem, and it can be worked out gradually, feeling the way carefully at each step forward. If the principle is recognized that no landed estates held by actual tillers of the soil should be taxed unless they are of an extent which can yield a net surplus, and that this surplus should be the basis of taxation, we may approach our ideal by graduated steps. A commission may be appointed to investigate and ascertain for each area what the extent of exemption should be. The smallest estates—say those of five acres and less—may be exempted first. At the same time, the high line of exemption in income-tax may be lowered so that some of the revenue foregone on land might be recouped from this source; and there is no unfairness in this equalization of the burden. This process of simultaneously raising the limit of exemption in land and lowering the limit of exemption in other items, may be gradually adopted till an equation is reached.

This policy should go hand in hand with a careful exploration of economy in public expenditure, and a toning up of efficiency in public investments and sources of income such as hydro-electric works, forests and industrial enterprises.

Problems of
Village Uplift

by
N. Kasturi

Enter any village. On the outskirts where the manure heaps are, you are received by a barrage of barks. The reception given by the animals is symbolic. The village wants, above all things, to be left alone.

The village has a deep suspicion of anyone from beyond, especially from the cities. 'Why don't you leave us alone?' the villagers seem to ask. 'You have taken away the food from the mouths of our artisans; you have sowed the seeds of intrigue and faction in our quiet and placid fields; you have robbed us of our best boys and planted schools to rob us of more; you have angered our gods and insulted our grand-fathers; you have built up an administrative machine operating in a devious, mysterious way. What new experiment in exploitation have you devised of late? Leave us alone,' they seem to say from behind their stony stares and effortful smiles.

Indeed, it is hard for the villagers to grasp the meaning of 'rural uplift' and the sincerity of 'rural service', when so much of it is still a stunt. Like mothers looking on when the young calves frisk about in glee, they watch the slogan-led enthusiast in amusement and in doubt. 'Have you no parents to keep you at home?' they inquire of the simple-minded visionaries froms school and college who sniff about in villages during vacations in order to improve sanitation. The wiseacres of the village—those who command its confidence and shape its future— shake their heads in silent disdain as the· reconstructors, after their morning 'cleaning campaign', jump on to their bicycles. They say, 'We have imbibed water from this very tank for a thousand years. And now these young colts tell us it is poison!' Or, 'We know this trick. Sure they are out for some mischief, for whoever heard of rich people's children sweeping the streets? They will either come back for contributions or subscriptions or free service; or, the gods will punish us for permitting this revolution. Oh! why did we ever agree to have that cursed approach road laid down!' Or, 'This year, Mari was so enraged that small-pox carried away hundreds of children, all because these upper-caste reformers insisted on entering the quarters of the untouchables.'

This last complaint may come from the untouchables themselves! For, they have been taught to believe in segregation as a divine dispensation. They fear the approach of the higher castes as much or even more than these latter are afraid of approaching them. Removal of the evils of untouchability is believed by many to depend upon a change in the outlook of the high-born. Of course, that is imperative. But by far the more urgent and the more difficult part of the problem lies in educating and inspiring the untouchables themselves. Their degeneration has been so long-standing that they have no desire to rise. Nor do they believe that it is ever possible for them to rise.

Village uplift service is, therefore, a question of re-forming patterns of thought and behaviour. It is a slow process, more lasting if more slow. A college student full of fanatic zeal for rural service reported after the summer recess, 'Sir, I had a lecturing tour through eight villages. They have all given up eating and drinking!' He meant that they had given up eating carcass and drinking toddy. Things don't move so quickly as that in rural India. There the pace is set by intimacy of contact and sincerity of purpose combined with obvious practical benefit. It is indeed very difficult for an outsider, not to speak of an 'educated city man', to establish such contact. The villager puts on a mask of inscrutability as a defence mechanism; or, he agrees with everybody and promises to do everything, all the while resolving to dodge as best as he can. The elephant, it is said, has two sets of teeth, one for show and the other for chewing.

Steeped in the atmosphere of a highly spiritualized civilization, the villager is bound to respond with great ease to all appeals in the name of religion. Herein lies great danger. The villager pays dearly today for his superstitions. He has to be persuaded out of them by the social worker who must have a great deal of tact and wise discrimination. It may be possible sometimes to explode a myth and thereby kill a superstition. In a certain village, people were afraid of a roadside rock which contained an ancient inscription. Some said that it was the devil's own script; others said that the writing indicated hidden treasure and quoted instances of men having been killed by thunderbolts when they, in their cupidity, dug under the rock to appropriate the gold. The inscription, however, was read by a social worker from college and the gods did not come out with their bolts! Literate villagers were induced to sit beside the rock and spell out the words for themselves. Luckily, the inscription mentioned the village by its present name, though it was written seven hundred years ago. It praised three donors belonging to the village thus: 'as truthful as Harischandra, as brave as Bhima and as generous as Karna'. So, the villagers became proud of the rock and were inspired to live up to the ideal of their own ancestors. Thus was the hidden treasure laid bare. A superstition will not always bear this kind of frontal attack. In such cases, they could be confronted with new truths in a different manner. A blind insistence on dry secularism is no good. Villagers have to be told that the same goddess or god who once demanded the sacrifice of goats and buffaloes to stop an infection of small-pox has now vouchsafed a new remedy suitable for the modern age of railways and buses and telegraphs and aeroplanes—namely, vaccination. In a certain village people refused to take quinine pills for malaria because they thought the recurrent fever was only the wicked prank of a demon that had to be appeased by a sacrifice. So, a new plan was devised when quinine had to be given in another village. The villagers were told that they were to take the pills facing east, on Tuesdays and Fridays after repeating thrice the name of God, because it was a Divine Gift to Man and so had to be swallowed with due ceremony. Dramatic performances in which divine beings, familiar to the villager, appear and recommend changed methods of life or new drugs or new foods will produce good effect.

The only advice which we can be sure the villager will take is that relating to his earning a few more coins. But, even here, the suggestion will be more easily accepted if it does not cut him away from his moorings and if it does not involve obvious risk. For, the villager has been too long exploited by men who give 'advice'. Like everyone else struggling for livelihood, he is severely practical, though he would fain stick to his village home itself. It is the same even in education. We appeal to the villager to send his children to school and there they learn to despise toil and to lisp a foreign tongue as a preliminary to the inevitable escape from the village life. The only schooling that would bring all the village children to the school is that which will not take away the farmhands from the fields and which will make them better behaved, healthier, and more useful. The standard of literacy for rural bridegrooms until a few years ago was the ability to read some good classic text in the language of the area and the *pial* school provided the facilities. Today, such eligibles can be counted on the fingers of one hand, even in big forward villages.

Those engaged in rural uplift have to remember that each village is a distinct individual. It has its own maladies and potentialities. Human and material resources vary; social and administrative traditions differ. A temple, a canal, a philanthropic sowcar, a bus-stop, a deep-rooted feud, each of these may create new problems. School hours, for example, may have to be varied according to the occupational needs of the people of each village. Uniform treatment of all villages will often be a waste of energy. 'A draw-well is more sanitary than a step-well,' says the slogan. So, the village was provided with a pucca well at great cost, forty feet deep, with crossbar and pulley complete. But, water was still being carried home from the condemned tank. 'Why not from the well? Is it not cleaner? Healthier?' we ask indignantly. 'Oh yes, it is cleaner,' we agree. 'But our mud pots will be broken if we let them down the well. We cannot afford the cost of pots. Besides, ropes are costly and have to be renewed twice a year,' is the reply.

The poverty of the villager trips us up in unexpected ways. It has cast a gloom over the whole countryside. The villager is almost always dejected and forlorn. Waves of laughter seldom ventilate their homes. Even the children grow up too soon. So, a great responsibility rests on all who crusade against 'wasteful extravagance' on occasions like birth, marriage, and death. Though individually every villager must be advised to live within his means, the rural worker must devise a calendar of village festivals which will appeal to all sections of the population. It is also noticeable that controversy is the very breath of village nostrils. Litigiousness has sapped the vitality of many families. In most cases, this is only the expression of the gambling instinct. Feuds and factions are also the manifestations of unsatisfied impulses towards pugnacity. The popularization of games among the younger men might alleviate the itch for dragging the other fellow to a court of law; it might also temper the acerbities of party factions, if vigilance is exercised to see that the competitive spirit does not run along communal lines and that the desire to win does not kill the very spirit and purpose of games.

The Indian village, again, has been a self-contained entity from time immemorial; its administrative problems have been handled by the elders on more or less successful lines. Each caste group has its own *Yajaman* or Master who lays down the law and interprets custom. In the name of the non-communal state and of Individualism, these institutions have been recently overshadowed by Panchayat councils elected on artificial urban principles. They are dominated by transient revenue officials. Something has to be done to adapt the new Panchayats to the old foundations of village government.

It will thus be seen that rural uplift service is no amateur's job. Nor are experts needed for it. It requires, above all, a sense of mission, an imaginative sympathy and an alert intellect. These are precious gifts vouchsafed only to the elect. But the rest of us can also put our shoulders to the wheel and help to push rural India on to the road of progress. Even the least of us can treat the villager a little more respectfully; bring a little more cheer to his home; help him to earn some more money; and recruit a new more sympathizers from among our friends.

Personal
Glimpses

A Meditation in Mid-Pacific

by
Paul Brunton, Ph.D.

I slipped into the snug canvas of a deck-chair which I had established on a lonely spot at the far end of the ship and watched the ocean spray dash twenty feet high and fling itself upon the smooth teakwood planks. The steamer, built a trifle too high amidships, reeled now and then and the chair with it. When I looked up into the sky's face, there was not the faintest slip of a moon, nor even one light from a pale star, but only a vast all-pervading and all-enveloping inky blackness, as impenetrable to the gaze as powdered onyx. The hushed stillness was broken by the rhythmic breathing of the cool tradewinds as they fanned the illimitable night, blew across the deserted decks and fluttered my clothes. The ship itself was like a fantastic ghost figure that moved mysteriously through a titanic mirage. Its bow cut into the water almost noiselessly.

Two hours earlier I had ascended from the dining-room. The captain of the ship had done the unexpected and undeserved honour of having me as a guest at his table throughout my stay on board. His conversation had taught me much about the mysteries of mid-ocean navigation and I had endeavoured to repay him by teaching a little about the mysteries of celestial navigation. Most of my instruction and even much of my conversation, however, were largely silent. Anyway, I hoped that both would bear an inevitable fruit and not many more voyages pass before he would begin to enquire how he might become, in Henley's famous phrase, the captain of his own soul instead of merely being the captain of somebody else's ship.

Here I was, I reflected, in mid-Pacific some forty degrees from land and forty centuries from the civilization of skyscraping cities. The curved hull of the ship was actually riding over the rocky giant's skeleton of that vanished archaic continent which the Tamil people call Gondwana, the Hawaians call Kahoopokane and the modern scientists Lemuria. I drank the wine of a curious languor, as I mused dreamily over the phenomenon of this incredible cemetery of mouldering continents and subcontinents lying mutely stretched and water-buried that was the

Pacific. The surviving unburied fragments which still remained—such as the Polynesian Archipelagoes, East Indian islands, Ceylon, South India, Aleutian Isles, Madagascar, Malaya, Sumatra, Australia and New Zealand—hardly hinted at the unbelievable extent of a land which had touched the African soil in the west and American soil in the east. Yet millions of human lives which it once supported were swept away by a stupendous fiery hurricane of subterranean eruptions and volcanic outbursts which seared and charred the earth amid cataclysmic earthquakes. Furious infernal fires, sulphurous smoke, acrid steam and poisonous gases filled the skies. Dante saw no grimmer vision of horror during his peregrinations of Purgatory. For the earth which seized and swallowed the human peoples into its flame-hissing mouth, was itself seized and swallowed by the great waters. Thus Nature, more thousands of years ago than history can conveniently record, finally washed away a stage which had outserved its purpose.

I let my thoughts play further around the same theme for in this watery solitude I was in a fit position to take an impartial view of the world at large.

What did this mean to humanity? The perspective of rolling centuries, the study of written history and the fragmentary revelations of pre-history would be worthless if they did not contain instruction for the living present. The fate of Lemuria constituted both a warning and a reminder to our own twentieth-century world. It was a dread warning that nothing material may abide with us for ever. The sufferings of the individual and the transitoriness of the world possessed a higher purpose than their immediate karmic one. They existed also to remind us that material existence was not our true home. When we were constantly made aware of the changeability of things and creatures, we eventually got tired of and dissatisfied with such existence and commenced to seek for something that would not change but be permanent, for something that was free from misery and disappointment. Such was the commencement of our initiation into the path to wisdom. Such was our first step towards finding the eternal changeless reality. It was also a mournful reminder of the frailty of human character, which had gone so far in the long passage of time since those misty Lemurian days, but so little in the awakening to awareness of its own spiritual source.

The night became somewhat chilly, so I turned up the collar of my coat and wrapped a blanket around my shoulders. The great bronze propellers swished quietly through the waves astern as the steamer sped over the dark waters. The utter isolation of its position on the world's largest and deepest ocean, which actually

contained more than half the earth's volume of
water, filled me anew with a sense of proper
perspective. I had taken a glance at the
antediluvian world; now I proposed to take a
glance at the contemporary world.

When, during the year before, I had been in
Europe it was plain for all to see that its
unfortunate inhabitants were merely waiting
for the cauldron of national greeds and racial
hates, narrow prejudices and ancient
selfishnesses to boil over into scalding war. It
was equally plain to see that the epoch which
had made Europe the leader of the West was
drawing amid much crisis and many convulsions
to a destined close. The European world was
trembling. It was afflicted with over-organization
in some parts and under-organization in others.
Its people were bewildered and its leaders were
afraid in their hearts. It was supposed to have
progressed but signs were a-plenty that this
progress was towards a precipice. Stupidity in
some high places straddled its form whilst
malignity in others was plotting devilish work.

When I was visiting Geneva and saw the
massive new buildings being completed for the
League of Nations, I said to a companion, 'There
is the birth of a great idea but the death of a
great hope. The League must perish because it
has put heads together but not hearts.'

War would come and come soon. Humanity
would bear ugly scars to tell of blurred vision

and mistaken choice; it would invite deep wounds by wrong action and cowardly inaction. No pact or peace treaty was nowadays worth the paper it was written on. Meanwhile men waited fatalistically with sinking heart and clouded brow, amid universal tension and universal fears, for the thunderclap of fratricidal war to strike upon the tympanum of the world's ear.

I had wandered the full circle around this melancholy globe of ours and could not recollect one country where there was no talk of this universal dread which touched every heart. Some felt this more lightly than others but there were lands where it hung like a thick oppressive fog over an entire nation. The Japanese professor who gravely shook his head over continuous cups of green tea in a Kyoto cafe, the Chinese officer who stood with his men on guard in a devastated countryside; the poor Indian peasant who lifted his bent back from the sun-baked field for a few minutes, the Arab sheikh who broke the desert silence by the powerful tones of his voice, the Sudanese negro trader who exchanged an ornate new leather belt for a few gadgets, the great connoisseur who displayed his priceless paintings in a gallery near the Place Vendome, the Viennese editor who sat amongst a mountain of papers piled on his desk, the shifty-eyed but sun-tanned adventurer who shared a compartment in a Hungarian train, the stockbroker who blew fragrant cigar smoke around the drawing-room of his London apartment, the American police detective who unhitched his pistol to sit in mystic meditation for fifteen minutes—all these betrayed dissatisfaction with the present epoch and their nervous fears of a war-clouded future soon after our talk had strayed from the first greetings.

When one surveyed the state of the world and made up a catalogue of the trials and tribulations and senseless stupidities that surrounded us, one could readily play the cynic and come to the quick conclusion that the only way to abolish the miseries of mankind was to abolish man.

Yet the tremendous area, imposing scale of tragedy and colossal mercilessness of what would be the most destructive of all wars would surely affect the minds of all mankind and arouse them for their habitual ethical torpor. The very uniqueness of the historic circumstances attending it would invite universal attention and foster some reflection thereon, however little. What else would it turn out to be but a bold and unforgettable demonstration of the fact that suffering was inseparably allied to life in this world? It was in fact forever with us, albeit on an unimpressive and unimposing scale—it was so familiar indeed that we tended to remain untouched by its normal existence. Only the extremely thoughtful who sought truth or peace took note of its ever-presence and sought also for some solution of its meaning or escape from its burden. Nevertheless, the agonizing calamity through which mankind would pass would daze people by its mechanized terror and modernized size. They might demand some explanation to still their perplexity. But alas! what lesson could be derived other than this age-old one which Buddha taught and Jesus gave?

In the ancient East there was still and in medieval Europe there was once a large class of men who found themselves *externally* in a roughly similar position. They were the wandering friars and roaming ascetics. They were men without home, property, family, money or career. Their position, however, was a voluntary one, for they renounced the conventional existence of this world because they had hopes of finding a better one. Thus they gained some measure of internal consolation from their external suffering. It was an existence of outer hardship but sometimes of inner peace. If genuine and not humbugs they learnt voluntarily what most mankind would be forced to accept involuntarily—the lesson of non-attachment.

It was not good for man to become so strongly attached to this earth that when the time came to part from it—whether suddenly or slowly—he raised a loud lament in surprise. And what was true of his physical life was equally true of his physical possessions. The element of destiny was forever at work in his midst. It played chess with his fortunes, his family, his property and his satisfactions. There was no more permanence here than there was in the length of his days. Nature was what she was. Wisdom lay in facing facts, not in ignoring them. And because one of the stupendous facts of life and property was that they were perishable, it behoved man to seek whilst he had the chance for a higher kind of life that should be imperishable and a superior kind of property which he could bear with him wherever he went. Hence war, man-made though it be, would also be a practical initiation of the whole world into this need of inner detachment.

After all, this world was but a contrivance to draw forth latent perfection; the situations in which we found ourselves and the social upheavals that surrounded us were but instruments to develop character and capacity, whilst the relations we contracted were the tests, temptations, opportunities and privileges to turn our possibilities into actualities. War was an awakener. It strained our characters to the utmost. Its stress and danger brought out both our hidden strength and disguised weakness. This enforced psycho-analysis was necessary if we were to make real and not sham progress. We might make alarming or assuring discoveries about ourselves, we might even find that we had been living in a world of make-believe, but in any case we would know better what we really were and what was the intrinsic worth of our social institutions. All this took time, and many were the earth-lives needed for its accomplishment. We needed therefore to be patient not only with ourselves but also with others, no matter how wicked they seemed to be. Life in the long run was a college of higher education where the apt pupils graduated more quickly but where the laggards were always given other chances.

Even totalitarian movements represented a violent and frantic reaction against the blindness of stupid governments or the weakness of cowardly ones, but it was a reaction whose fundamental unreason only delayed and could not stop the advance of decent civilized society. If war was catastrophic for the individual, it was also a catalyser for society in general.

All that warred against human unity, that would turn the hand of man against his brother, would one day infallibly perish. None of us dared hope to see such a day, for quick milleniums were the cheap delusions of wishful thinkers, but all of us might hope to find within overselves *even now* that same sacred principle and thus assure ourselves of its truth. We might safely take our stand on the oneness of essential being. We could wait quietly for the Infinite Mind to reclaim its own progeny. We must endeavour to aspire meanwhile toward that region where the atmosphere was timeless.

One need not lose heart, therefore. No single defeat and no violent devolution was really definite in the more ancient war of light against night.

Hope was the beautiful message of the unknown goal, the star that blazed when all else was dark, the encouragement of the sublime Perfect to the struggling imperfect. It was the unconscious turning of the flower to the sun. It bestowed strength on the weak and endurance on the sorrowful. It was a way up from flinty tracts to the level plateau where the worst troubles vanished. And those of us who had planted their feet on the grander path that led to ultimate wisdom, had to go on, whether it be through sorrow or joy, weakness or strength, world-turmoil or world-peace. For us there was no turning back.

The sun darted its early rays across the horizon. Dawn had come. I awoke with a sudden start. Huddled in the chair, I had slept throughout the night. The terminus of my meditation had let me pass into that other dimension of being which is sleep. I got up and walked to the handrail, lingering there to watch the white curls of foam swirling and churning upon the angry waves. A few frolicsome dolphins disported themselves thus early in the day, following the wake of the ship as it slid pleasantly along.

Waves of orange and mauve colour spread

over the sky as the sun gave a watery world its benign greetings. The ship's smoke crawled skywards out of the funnels and offered a black contrast. How far from the world's folly and stupidity, hatred and passion were these waxing beams which were soon to glow with friendly warmth! How grand was this solar message! For as the sun's beams had eventually broken through the night's heavy darkness, so might we hope that when Time, that dread figure with the scythe of death, came sweeping near us his strokes could not touch this truth: that if man would listen in silent reverie to the rare and subtle intimations of his hidden being, he would one day find his heart put under enchantment and his brain made mute, the while an indefinable peace and indescribable love proclaimed that something unearthly dwelt within and about him.

A Visit to Kashmir and Ladakh

by

W.G. Eagleton

It was my good fortune to spend the hot weather
of this year, in the company of Mr Peter Wright
of Bangalore, in Kashmir and Ladakh. When I
say the hot weather, I mean of course the hot
weather of Mysore. In Ladakh at that time, at
the altitudes we reached, temperatures were
down to twelve degrees, and in the rather
primitive dak bungalows of the grandiloquently-
named Treaty High Road, which leads from
Srinagar to Leh and Yarkand, and beyond to
Kashgar and Urumchi, we drank our steaming
Ovaltine at night by the light of the flickering
hurricane lamp that our coolies had hauled up
the pass, and retired to bed cowering under six
blankets and heavy dressing-gowns, with our

wooden cots drawn up as close as possible to a roaring log fire. Even then, too often we lay awake shivering.

I doubt if I can say anything new or profound about the widely-canvassed beauties of Kashmir proper. The Kashmir Tourist Bureau does justice to those. Everyone has heard Srinagar called the Venice of the East. Everyone has heard of that rich and lovely valley, which Tom Moore could describe without ever having seen it, because it is the imperishable type of the happy valley. Everyone knows of the formal beauties of Srinagar, with its terraced Mughal gardens and its graceful quasi-Venetian shikaras, propelled by highly-respectable but unmistakably Semitic gondoliers over the surface of glamorous and filthy canals. At every turn, squalor tempered by magnificence, the vista of the grubby bazaar-street terminating in the unapproachable Himalayan snows, a very un-bourgeois paradise. And then the ruffianly touts, offering carved walnut, papier-mache, pashmina ring-shawls and gems from Central Asia, sometimes wheedling, sometimes almost threatening, but always dogging us with a persistence only to be rivalled perhaps by the fly-whisk-selling dragomans of Port Said. For Srinagar is tourist-ridden these days. One would hate to be called a travel-snob, but I feel that with the best will in the world one could not call Srinagar unspoiled. Baedeker's famous characterization of the inhabitants of the European continent as 'always extortionate and often abusive' came frequently into the mind. Yet Srinagar has character, with the big brick-built sham-Tudor villas, incongruously Victorian and English and suburban, and then again the tall grass growing on the roofs of the houses, the brilliantly-plumaged exotic birds, the fakir who knelt down on the crown of the road, and laid his forehead nine times to the ground, indifferent to the shrieking of motor-horns and the vituperation of jutka-wallahs. One leaned from the balcony of one's hotel and watched the infinite variety of the street-life. One leaned to pick out the Brahmin in his Jodhpur breeches and pale-pink turban, the middle-class Muslim in his smart European suit and his arrogant gaudy puggaree, perched like a silk hat on a Bradford millionaire; and out-numbering these, the poorer Muslim peasant with pointed clogs and tapering pyjamas, a coarse heavy blanket thrown about his shoulders and his close-fitting brown skull-cap on his head, often jogging up the middle of the road on an undersized mountain pony with bridle and stirrups of string or hay-rope. And many a reminder there was as we noticed with a thrill that Srinagar is the starting-place of the great caravan route that leads into Central Asia, the brightly-coloured Chinese cap of a Yarkandi merchant, or the ankle-length maroon coat and white cummerbund of a lama. And we began to understand the question that was so often put to us in Srinagar; when did you leave India?

But to us Srinagar was only the stepping-off place for Ladakh, and we came eventually to look upon it, sometimes on my part with more than a touch of nostalgia, as the metropolis of sophistication, and of the blasé fastidious culture upon which we had turned our backs. I had better say a few words about the route into Ladakh, the famous Treaty High Road. The Treaty High Road into Central Asia was made passable for peaceful caravans by the efforts of Colonel Durand's column in 1891, and as far as the frontiers of Turkestan it is maintained and supervised jointly by the British Government and the Government of Kashmir. Elaborate arrangements are made for the provision of transport and supplies to authorized travellers along the route, but as we found to our cost, these arrangements do not and cannot function perfectly in winter time, when travellers are not expected, the road being officially closed, and when the good people of Ladakh are hard put to it to get enough to eat for themselves. By what is known as the Res system, each group of villages along the route is obliged to provide transport at fixed rates, up to a certain limit. For instance, the large village of Dras can be distrained upon to the extent of twenty coolies and eighty ponies or zo, a zo being a cross between a cow and a yak. But in early April,

when we set out, the route is quite impassable
to ponies or to zo or to any other four-footed
beast, so that our little caravan actually
consisted, most of the time, of a straggling line
of laden coolies, who in the course of a day's
march, clambering over the ice-bound slopes,
each man fending for himself, inevitably got
strung out over a distance of some miles. Peter,
who was invariably the first to make the.rest-
house, usually had to wait for several hours
before the last man had reported. I was quite
frequently the last man. At each resthouse a
contractor, or *thekedar*, had undertaken to supply
provisions at fixed rates, and as we glanced
down the lists kindly furnished by the British
Joint Commissioner in Srinagar—butter 1/8 per
seer, fuel 10 annas per maund, green grass 8
annas per maund, dry grass one rupee per
maund, sheep (alive) three seers per rupee,
chicken 8 annas each, fowl 14 annas, eggs 6
annas per dozen, milk 3 annas per seer—we
told ourselves that whatever the difficulties and
perils encountered, at least we should not want
for something to put in the hollow tooth.

'Oh, blindness to the future, kindly given,
That each may fill the circle mark'd by
Heaven!'

What we had heard however of the great Zojila
Pass, nearly twelve thousand feet up, between
Kashmir and Ladakh, filled us with far greater

trepidation. George Roerich, who crossed the Zojila Pass in 1925 with the Roerich Central Asian Expedition, writes: 'It presents no difficulty in late summer or autumn, but in winter it is dangerous, and practicable only for men, for its avalanche-swept slopes are covered with ice and snow which may at any time give way and carry the traveller down the precipice. Traffic is closed for the whole of winter and during early spring, during which time the traveller has to pay double rates to the coolies who agree to face the peril on the summit of the pass.' At the time when we set out Ladakh and Zojila were still in the grip of winter, and the road was officially impassable. The British and Kashmir Joint Commissioners, whose written permission was necessary before we could embark upon the journey, were anything but encouraging; the British Joint Commissioner in particular, the Chota Resident Sahib, painted a lively picture of the terrors before us, and tried hard to interest us in the less recondite attractions of Gulmarg and Pahalgam. He made it clear that permission could not be given unless we were accompanied by an experienced guide, and so for three days in the company of our good friend Mr Gulam Mohiyuddin, we trudged from one caravanserai to another trying to find some Central Asian trader to whose caravan we could attach ourselves. In the Tibetan serai of Srinagar, a tumble-down forsaken place, we found only a

poor old Tibetan lying fever-stricken upon a bed
of rags on the rough earthen floor of the serai,
with the ponies of his companions tethered beside
him. We gave him a little money, and Mr Gulam
Mohiyuddin arranged for medicines to be sent
to him, but we found there no other sign of life
and could get no tidings of any caravan starting
for Ladakh at that time of year. In the Yarkandi
serai, a much more prosperous place, a number
of Central Asian traders, bearded, slant-eyed,
Mongolian Muslims in figured Chinese robes,
cut off from their homes and families by the
closing of the Russian frontier, had spread their
Bokhara carpets on the floor, and feathered cosy
little nests for themselves wherein to await the
coming of better times; but no one thought of
setting out for Ladakh for at least some weeks,
and we could not afford to wait. Moreover,
estimates of the cost of the proposed journey
varied bewilderingly, and even the lowest
estimate was disconcerting enough. At last,
through the good offices of Mr Gulam
Mohiyuddin, we were introduced to a wealthy
Yarkandi merchant, Mahomed Umar Khan, who
was even then assembling a large caravan for
the journey to Leh. Mahomed Umar Khan, very
Muslim in manner and feature, very Chinese in
dress, was an old gentleman of extraordinary
personal dignity and courtliness—to this day it
is one of my regrets that I failed to get a
photograph of him—and the prospect of having

him as a travelling companion was enormously
reassuring to me, the more so as the obvious
comfort of his house in Srinagar, his urbanity
and evident appreciation of the good things of
life, made me feel that the rigours of the journey
must have been greatly exaggerated. Moreover,
as we afterwards learnt, he had accompanied
the Roerich Central Asian Expedition as far as
Kashgar. His language was Turki and he could
speak no English, but with the help of Peter's
halting Urdu we made ourselves understood,
and an arrangement highly satisfactory to us
was arrived at. But the question was now
whether we could be ready in time, for Umar
Khan was impatient to start. Then followed
three feverish days when we rushed distractedly
about Srinagar, purchasing camp-beds, tin
kettles and eating utensils, long alpenstocks,
puttees, blankets, grass shoes, woollen caps and,
as it seemed to us, all the paraphernalia of a
Polar expedition. It made things no easier for us
that all these purchases had to be made
conditional upon our finally getting permission
to go, for the Chota Resident Sahib had not yet
brought himself to the point of signing the
order. And when at length, at our final visit to
his office, with a shrug of his shoulders and a
'Well, you seem to be determined about it,' he
put his signature to the document, and obtained
from us a written assurance that we would not
attempt to cross into Turkestan; by the time all

these formalities were completed, Umar Khan, to our great disappointment, had been obliged to start without us. However, he was only a day ahead of us, and he promised to wait for us at Gund, two days' march from Srinagar. But floundering in that deep snow we were never able to overtake him; for some time we continued to receive messages which he left for us with villagers on the way, but after two or three days we gave up the pursuit. We never saw Umar Khan again, and had to make the best of our way without him, thus losing the credit of having accompanied the first caravan to get across the Zojila pass this year.

Two days brought us to Sonamarg, 8,600 feet up, and for most of the way we tramped through pastoral country reminiscent of the Vale of Llangollen in North Wales. A pleasant, fertile valley, a meandering country road between 'dry walls' of loose, piled-up stones; beneath us the rushing Sindh river, crossed here and there by a rickety wooden bridge, and on each side the green slopes of the lower hills; ponies and goats grazing everywhere, even actually on the roofs of the village houses; peasants and shepherds recalling in their irrepressible friendliness the peasants of Ireland, brushing aside with a cheerful 'Salaam, sahib', the much-misconstrued diffidence of the Englishman. But within a few miles of Sonamarg we found ourselves floundering in several feet of snow. I remember sitting down for half an hour to rest on the top of a mile post, which said, I think, two miles to Sonamarg. On our return journey, after the snow had cleared away, I was shocked to find that I could not even reach the top of that mile-post. From then onwards, we occasionally stumbled upon the top of a telegraph pole, and that was all we ever saw of the Treaty High Road. At Sonamarg we camped in the serai, the other half of which was occupied by a deliciously dirty and picturesque Tibetan family, carrying their children slung on their backs like the Esquimeaux. And here we changed into our winter kit, Jodhpur breeches and puttees, belted mackintoshes, woollen Balaclava helmets pulled down over our shoulders, sun-glasses, fur gloves and long sharp-pointed staves. Over our stout boots we drew the grass shoes that are worn by the coolies in the snow, and of which one may expect to wear out two pairs a day. I should add that the intense cold made it quite impossible to shave, with the result that each day I looked more and more like the Second Murderer out of *Macbeth*. As for our coolies, six in number, it is said of the Tibetans that they never take a garment off once it has been put on; when it begins to fall to pieces another garment is put on over it; and the bulky amorphous figures of our coolies would seem to give colour to this belief.

Another day's difficult march brought us to

Baltal, at the foot of the pass, the dak bungalow half buried in snow and ringed round with a pine forest, all the ingredients of a Northern European Christmas, and above us, to the south-west, the glistening pyramid of Mount Amarnath. Now we were really up against it. To the Machoi bungalow, on the other side of the pass, is only ten miles, but the pass can be crossed only on foot, only in fine weather, and only at night, and it is a whole night's journey. During the day-time a howling wind springs up, which does not make the precipices any safer, or add to one's feeling of security; moreover, when the sun gets up the avalanches begin. What is perhaps even worse, the sunrise brings a softening of the surface of the snow which makes the going ten times more laborious. In fact, for this reason, we consistently tried to avoid travelling by day. At every step one sinks in up to the thigh, and must drag one's leg painfully out and plunge it in again, an effort not made any the easier by the great altitude and consequent strain upon the heart. Even then, of course, one has not touched dry ground, and one never knows how much deeper one may sink at the next step. And on all sides, as far as the two lines of peaks that run along both sides of the route, nothing but snow. Nothing to sit on, nothing to lean against, nothing to clutch at, so that it is impossible ever to rest. Usually, after setting out before daybreak, we had no food until we reached our shelter for

the night, sometimes a stretch of twelve hours.
For we invariably underestimated the time taken
for the day's march, and once having set out we
could not stop; in fact with the sun getting
higher every hour and occasionally the noise of
an avalanche crashing behind us, we dared not
stop, though we were unable to make any better
speed. When we became thirsty we used to
break off an icicle and eat it. Every day our feet
were wet to the skin, in spite of our precautions,
and when we finally reached our resting-place,
the hours that remained to us before turning in
were always spent in attempting to dry our
clothes and shoes before the fire.

I remember how we got up that morning in
Baltal, the unearthly hour and the oppressive
solitude of our surroundings giving us the
sensation of getting up to be hanged, groping for
our things in the half-light and packing them by
the glow of the dying log-fire. As we started out
in a long file for the conquest of Zojila, the clear
light of the moon threw our shadows against the
great wall of snow and gave us, with our woollen
helmets and long lance-like poles, the silhouette
of crusaders. While we scrambled up the pass in
the dark, with nothing to afford us a foothold,
not a rock, not a branch, nothing to clutch with
the hand, nothing but the slippery hardened
surface of the snow, we became afflicted with a
nervous loquacity; we discussed, as I remember,
the validity of Anglican orders, labouring the

most obvious and irrelevant points with a feigned nonchalance, and with many a scared glance at the vertiginous slopes above. By 10 am we reached the safety and comparative warmth of the Machoi bungalow, and knew that the worst was behind us. But I confess to many an uncomfortable moment in Ladakh whenever I remembered the appalling snow-covered precipice which we had put between us and civilization.

At Metaiyan our elderly cook became ill; and after allowing him to retard our progress for some days, we eventually had to leave him behind with a little money, to be picked up on our way back. Henceforward we had to fend for ourselves in the matter of cooking also, which indeed was not so difficult as it sounds, for we could get precious little to cook. At Dras we were able to secure the services of a stalwart Ladakhi called Gulam Mahomed, who proved a cheerful and willing worker but unfortunately knew no more of cooking than we were able to teach him ourselves; and thereafter the monotony of our food became a great trial. At Dras we rested for several days, receiving many kindnesses from the friendly postmaster, who insisted that it was his obligation as a public servant to cook for us when we could make no other provision; a versatility and a conception of duty as rare as it is laudable among our civil servants. By this time the snows had begun to melt somewhat, and slush rather than snow

was the element in which we now lived. On the
return from Dras, starting as usual well before
daybreak, I was actually able to use a pony for
a short distance; but after a few miles the snow
became both deeper and softer as day broke and
we got nearer to the summit of the pass, so that
at every few yards the surface would break and
either the forelegs or the hindlegs of my steed
would abruptly sink in a foot and a half. As the
precipices were uncomfortably near I dared not
risk being thrown, and after persevering for a
little way I resorted once again to Shanks' pony.

At Machoi, on our way back, came our great
adventure, when we were held up for three days
by a snowstorm which made it impossible for us
to venture further. The telegraph line had been
broken by an avalanche nearby—not that it
would have done any good to send telegrams, for
no one could reach us there—and the postal
runners, carrying the mail down to Srinagar,
were also snowed up with us, so that there were
about twelve of us in all. At Machoi there is no
village, only an isolated timber hut at the wind-
swept summit of Zojila, and consequently there
were no supplies of food whatever, except for the
little that we carried with us. The nearest village
on the Ladakh side is six miles away, and only
once did the storm abate sufficiently to enable
one of our men to go in search of food. After an
absence of the greater part of a day he came
back with a few eggs and a very small quantity

of milk. Fortunately the coolies had a bag of maize-flour, with which they made chapattis and shared them with us. On the second day we had to ration ourselves to one chapatti, one egg and one potato for each meal, and we allowed ourselves three such meals in the day—and very unappetizing they were. All day long we could do nothing but sit huddled before our fire in our overcoats, and read some old and ragged copies of *Blackwood's Magazine* which the chowkidar had unearthed. And every few minutes we looked anxiously at the sky for signs of better weather. One of my most vivid memories is of waking each morning at 3 or 4 am, and seeing the great bulk of Gulam Mahomed in the doorway against the phosphorescent snow, and listening in the darkness to the dialogue that took place every morning between him and Peter. '*Asman saf hai*? (Is the sky clear?)' And when Gulam Mahomed replied that it was not, I was secretly almost relieved, in spite of the hardships we were enduring, to know that I need not renew my acquaintance with Zojila yet awhile. Finally, on the third morning, when all our food was exhausted, the postal runners woke us in the small hours, and gave it as their opinion that if we made haste we might risk the descent of the pass. We crossed it, thank Heaven, without mishap, and after that made double speed back to Srinagar, and to the good food and comfortable beds of our hotel. And in a few days' time we

were busily looking through the back numbers
of the newspapers, and taking up again the
burden, the 'anguish and doubt and fear and
sorrow and pain', of this unhappy war-racked
world.

The Road to Mercara

(A Travel Diary)
by
M.N. Srinivas

I left Mysore by the Mail Bus. The weather was
cool, with a pleasant wind blowing from the
west. In front of me sat a boy of about ten
years—a very dark boy who wore green
spectacles that were too large for him. He was
reading a newspaper through his green glasses.
By his side was a Muslim dressed in multi-
coloured clothes. It was Ramzan, and probably
the Muslim was going home to his people. In the
same row occupying the last seat was a hefty
fellow in a woollen suit. He wanted to talk to
me, but I was in no mood for it. I am always
moody at the beginning of a journey. A kind of
mild melancholy fills me at such times. I feel a
sentimental attachment to the things I am

leaving behind. Something or other now reminded me of my college days. It was evening, the hour between day and night. There was the cricket field stretching away before me, and the slender tower of the pavilion stood outlined against a sky, rendered ineffably beautiful by a dying sun. The players threw long, slanting shadows on the green-carpeted floor, and the sun lit up everything with a mild, golden light. The scene rose up before me, and I was filled with a strange melancholy. Why was man born? What was the purpose of all this beauty? And why should you be compelled to leave your friends and relatives behind you and go about in a bus?

We had an uneventful journey up to Hunsur. There (at the entrance to the town, to be exact) the Muslim suddenly shook himself out of sleep and exclaimed, 'I have lost my purse! I have lost twenty-five rupees!' And then he became inarticulate, producing gurgles and making wild gestures which had meaning only for himself. He pointed to the boy with the green spectacles and said, 'He . . . he saw . . . my purse . . .' 'You . . . monkey!' he shouted at the boy. It was hardly believable. Such a young fellow to have done it! 'Search the boy. He must have it on him if he has stolen it.'

'Search him!' the cry was taken up by the entire bus. The boy remained surprisingly cool and said, 'Search me if you like!' He proceeded to strip. The Muslim gripped the boy's arm and moaned. 'My money gone!' 'Look into your coat pocket,' said a friendly voice, but he refused to do anything but moan. Suddenly, out of the confusion, I saw the conductor hold up a purse, saying, 'I have it! I found it under the seat!' Then the whole bus turned on the boy. 'We will give him over to the police!' 'He ought to be tied to a post and whipped!' 'His grandfather is a big merchant here, in Hunsur. He has a lakh of rupees. And look what a grandson he has!' 'He is certain to become a big robber one day.'

I ventured to say, 'Threaten the boy that you will hand him over to the police, and let him alone after a drubbing.' The conductor was practical. 'We shall have to wander to and fro the court if we tell the police.' This settled it. But someone shouted from behind, 'Don't tell him that now. Give him a good fright now, or when he grows up, he will rob our homes.' This message was accepted by everyone. 'We are handing you over to the police,' everyone told the boy. The driver also joined in the joke. He stopped the bus in front of the police station and shouted, 'Be quick with it. It's late already.' The boy was now convinced that the driver meant business. His stony calm was at last broken. He wept profusely: 'Anything but the police. Sirs, I will hold your feet and beg your pardon. I promise never to do such a thing again.' The conductor kicked him. I threatened the boy, 'I will send word to your grandfather.' The boy held my feet, 'Do anything but give me to the police.' The bus left the police station and his weeping stopped as suddenly as it had started. The bus at last halted in front of the Hunsur Post Office. Someone thrashed the boy soundly. He was ably assisted in the task by the postmaster, the peons, and in fact, by everyone who passed that way at the moment. Truly, we are a moral people, and everyone who had a whack at the boy was doing so purely out of moral considerations!

A few miles from Hunsur. It was a scrub jungle. The gentleman in the woollen suit made up his mind to talk to me: 'Are you bound for Mercara?'

'Yes.'

'Then nove on to my side, and we can talk.' He assumed I was eager to talk to him. His friend, a Coorg, who had just returned from Bangalore after an interview with the Recruiting Officer, joined in the conversation.

I told them who I was. I was writing a thesis on the Coorgs for Bombay University. Yes, it was my first journey to Coorg. I didn't know a soul there. I had a letter of introduction to someone.

Immediately, Bhim Sigh (for that was his name) took charge of me. He told me what to see there and what not to. The Coorg added his own comments now and then.

Bhim Singh was a Rajput. He was born in Mercara. His ancestors had moved down south from Central India. He spoke Kodagi like a Coorg. He had married a Kodagi girl. At present he was in Bangalore, doing business. He had, from what I heard of him, led a varied life. He had been contractor, travelling salesman, and a hundred other things. He had roamed all over India. He was in Bombay for three years, and a year in Ceylon. Now he was on his way to Mercara because his mother was dead.

I said 'Sorry.'

She was old. Sixty-five. But a mother, however old she is, is a mother. Bhim Singh hadn't seen her for ten years.

We approached the Mysore border. The narrow road ran through the thick and high jungle.

'Any game here?' I asked.

'Of course. Everything. I have shot any number of deer. And cheetahs are pretty common.'

'Any tigers?'

'Tigers! I once shot two in a day here. I used to camp here in a lorry every night from Mercara. That was years ago. We got news that a tiger had killed a cow here. We sat up over the kill. Nothing happened till four in the morning. It was very cold and our teeth chattered. We decided to go away. As we tried to get down the tree, two tigers, a male and a female, appeared suddenly, and we shot them both. I will show you the skins at Mercara.'

The jungle was denser. Bamboo shot up to a height of fifty or sixty feet. The bamboo is a most graceful tree. High above on the trees, graceful fronds bowed, swaying in the breeze, to the deities of the jungle.

The Coorg invited me to his estate. It was near Siddapur. 'Of course, you will find it pretty dull. I wouldn't have invited you if you were here for pleasure.'

Bhim Singh told me he had some good books about the Coorgs. 'I will give them to you. Meet me at the bus-stand tomorrow. I would have met you earlier, but for the funeral.'

'It doesn't matter. Thank you.'

'I will arrange about your food also. And I will take you to Uttaiah. He knows a lot about Coorg. And you must come to Bangalore. My wife can tell you a good many things.'

I thanked him once again.

Siddapur. The Coorg took leave of us. I saw him disappear into the jungle along a footpath, followed by a servant carrying his trunk.

Siddapur is a village on a slope. Pigs and hens cross the street causing the driver a good deal of annoyance. The houses were thatched with straw. The rain and sun of months had painted the straw a dull grey. Mercara is nearly two thousand feet above Siddapur, and the distance between the two is only twenty miles.

The ascent is steep. Silver oak trees shoot up to a great height on either side of the road. Pepper vines with their broad, dark leaves—I mistook them for betel—wind themselves round the stately silver oak. Below these spread the coffee plants, their dark-green, shining leaves looking strangely vicious. The oak trees look very respectable, guardians of the hoary traditions of a dead age. And like all those who stand for the past, they are more than a trifle gloomy.

The climb was steep. We reached a town having the unique name of 'The Tenth Mile', the tenth mile from Mercara. Bhim Singh was engaging someone, who had entered the bus at Siddapur. 'I smoke a hundred cigarettes a day. And I offer fifty to businessmen. It's all necessary in business. Often I leave tins with those likely to give me business. That's the right way in business.'

Meanwhile, the bus sped along a snake-like way up a hill. The tarred road was narrow, cut out of a niggardly hill. On one side the ground fell in an abrupt slope a thousand feet or so. Coffee twigs trailed into the road, waving a welcome. A hill rose on the other side. Before us, we saw a green wall of trees. When the bus reached the green wall, it turned sharply to a side and went round the hill. To our left was a great green valley flecked with brown. Beyond this stood a clear blue hill against a cloud-filled sky. In the centre of the valley ran a paddy field, like a tender-green river and lost itself in a dark jungle of tall trees. On the other bank of the paddy-river stood a red house.

It was all a riot of green. Ferns, beautiful and delicate, grew on the wayside.

Mercara. A strange town it looks from the bus, red-roofed houses pasted on to the slope of a hill. The houses clung together, like men on a cold night. Mercara looks a toy-town, pretty as a picture.

The policeman at the bus-stand told Singh where his mother was buried. Singh became moody, and for the first time in the journey silent. I shook hands with him, and promising to meet him the next day, got down from the bus.

The main street in Mercara goes up a hill. It looks fantastic to men of the plains. The climb was a stiff one. Why did the houses huddle so closely?

I reached my destination. My host was out on his weekly visit to the estate. The hostess told me to wait for a few minutes while she prepared coffee for me. It started raining outside. I felt lonely. 'Six months I have to spend in this place,' I thought with some bitterness.

Suddenly, I recollected Girgaum. Girgaum, that synonym for dirt and noise and crowd—I felt a homesickness for it. The trams and buses going their noisy way, men and women jostling one another for want of space. The brilliant neon signs, hoots of motor horns, the cries of *gharry wallahs*—in short, the crowded and brilliant life that flows through that vein of Bombay. I hungered for it. Solitude and loneliness are attractive to those who don't know either; I told myself. The beauty of a crowd on Chowpatty sands—I felt I would not exchange it for all the beauty of nature.

Sketches from Life

by
R.K. Narayan

Every artist has his own rough sketch-book in which he puts down passing figures and scenes that catch his eye. It is not always done with a utilitarian motive. He may find a use for these sketches on a future occasion or he may never look at them again. A novelist or a story-teller too has a similar sketch-book, in which he records his impressions. He is chiefly interested in human nature and its environment, and their interplay. He is ever watching his fellow-beings and classifying and labelling them. This may appear to be a very discreditable piece of work to do, but it cannot be helped. It is an occupational habit.

The sketch in the writer's album may be an elaborate analysis or it may be a mere enumeration of a few characteristics, with

emphasis on eccentricities, which are as high-
lights in a nature. There need not be any plan
or pattern in the sketch as there is in a story.

I keep an album of this kind, and in these
pages I shall present some of my studies, one or
more at a time. These are all based on actual
observations, although the names are fictitious.

* * *

I shall begin with a person called Gopal, B.A.
He is a man who lives and works in our midst
but whose ambition is (or rather was) to make
his mark on English Literature. He is today
nearing forty. His ambition to be a writer started
when he was less than seventeen. Let us go
back to an evening in those far-off days. Gopal
notices the sunset, nearly for the first time. The
still hour, the magic of the dusk, the illumined
clouds, and the river Sarayu winding away with
a chatter—the harmony of the hour suddenly
overwhelms him. He goes home, takes a piece of
paper, and writes several lines beginning: 'Oh,
the sunset . . .' There are far too many 'Oh's in
it, and he hasn't said anything in these lines
which others haven't already said. But this
performance pleases him greatly; he treasures
that scrap of paper. His aesthetic sense has
awakened and it has naturally found expression
in literary effort; this, particularly at adolescence,
is an inevitable law of nature as water flowing
down a slope or buds blossoming into flowers.

After being written about, an experience acquires a fresh quality, a new richness. This is another natural law in operation: literature enriching experience. Hence, from this moment the sunset is something different from what it was yesterday. Gopal notices new colours, forms, disposition of the clouds and harmonies. He notices, too, moonlight, feminine form, flowers, lightning and thunder, and the bird whistling on a branch. As far as this simple soul is concerned these things have come into existence for the first time. And everything is duly recorded on paper.

He treasures these bits of paper carefully in his table drawer, reads them aloud to himself every now and then, finds their sound exhilarating, and feels convinced that these are masterpieces of literary composition.

Presently an occasion comes for him to watch, at close-quarters, death. His friend's father is dead. And Gopal catches, as a radio catches ether waves, the grief and bewilderment of another. Emotion has awakened. It is just once removed (a friend's) to save him the hopelessness of a personal tragedy, and yet not so far off as to leave him untouched. He dwells in the luxury of this sorrow and late in the night writes an *In Memoriam* apostrophizing Death. This gives him a peculiar relief, and literature as usual enriches life, so that after being written about even death appears somewhat softened. He sits down and polishes his *In Memoriam* till he can touch it no more.

And then comes along his friend. One does on an evening walk get into a confiding mood, and out come the poems. This friend is very good. He has the poems read to him on the river bank by the light of the setting sun. He listens and shakes his head appreciatively as if he listened to music. He is the model of what a poet's public ought to be. 'Beautiful, beautiful,' he says and asks, 'why don't you send these to a paper? They will surely print these and pay you. I know a fellow in our place who gets ten or fifteen rupees for everything he writes . . .' Now the seeds of mischief are sown. Gopal gives his compositions to a typist, who, with a new ribbon and wide margins, makes these poems look like little masterpieces. He presents a bill for two or three rupees, and Gopal's pocket-money for the coming month is already mortgaged. The typed sheets go by next day's post to a famous newspaper office in Madras, accompanied by an elaborate letter from the poet, explaining, cajoling, and appealing. Castles go up in the air. Gopal entirely thrives on the quiet thrill of this vision till the postman brings back all the poems one morning, the manuscripts slightly crumpled and creased under the touch of unfriendly editorial fingers. The little printed slip pinned to the manuscripts says. 'The editor regrets his inability to use the enclosed

manuscripts owing to pressure on his space . . .'
Space! Space! What hypocrisy to complain of
lack of space! He and his friend look through
that day's newspaper and realize what an
amount of space is squandered criminally all
over. Here they might have omitted that cycle
theft, and there the reception to the retiring
executive engineer, and in another corner the
results of a fourth-rate football tournament, and
no one would groan with disappointment if that
horrible lecture on primary school problems were
reduced to two lines from fifty-two. If all that
space were saved, poems could certainly be put
in without inconveniencing any one. So thinks
Gopal, and his friend is in complete agreement.
The serenity of creative satisfaction is now rudely
shaken by factors like fame and fortune. For,
apart from its intrinsic worth or otherwise every
literary effort has a subjective value to a writer.

A certain amount of bitterness and anxiety
has now crept into Gopal's life. The poems go to
another editor and to another and another and
yet another. Every coin that comes into the
young man's pocket goes as postage. He is now
very familiar with the ways and manners of
editors. He can write a thesis on the different
styles in which editors reject proffered
contributions. Meanwhile he has also been
reading much. He makes the disconcerting
discovery that *Palgrave's Golden Treasury*
contains many poems on the very subjects on

which he himself has written. Nine out of ten persons, after this discovery and under the pressure and distractions of life which makes their presence felt at the period between adolescence and youth, would put their poems away, and not worry about the matter again in their lifetime. But Gopal has in him the stuff of a literary workman. He has persistence and nearly indestructible hope. Discouragements and disappointments make him temporarily unhappy but do no permanent damage.

He writes unceasingly. He realizes that editors do not at all want poems. They favour prose. And forthwith he changes over to prose. Well might the muses bewail this desertion all eternity, but that is none of his concern. 'I shall write poetry for my own pleasure but I will address the public only in prose,' he confides to his friend. He is completely thrilled by this discovery of his mistake. He sits down at night with sheets of paper before him. He has necessarily to take up this work late in the night, because he is without peace of mind unless he studies for two hours his college texts. The night is silent. Everyone at home has gone to bed; the paper is smooth, the nib is sharp, the mind is tranquil: everything is perfect and ready—except a subject. He sits nibbling the pen for a long while, and nothing happens. He feels rather sleepy and is about to get up and go to bed. And suddenly flashes the idea 'Write on the search for a subject'. And there goes a confession on paper for all the world to see. This essay begins, 'It is nearly eleven at night and the snores of my brothers and parents reach me while I sit struggling here with paper and pencil. What shall I write about?' He strikes the pose of an utterly bewildered man into whose head stream a hundred subjects for an essay: Swarajya, Relativity, World Situation, the Neighbour's Puppy, and so on. He considers them one by one and dismisses them with an euphemistic confession of ignorance of each subject. And this fills up six pages. He goes to bed in peace. The first thing he does as soon as he is up next morning is to read over what he has written. He finds it a sparkling performance. He never knew he had in him such an abundance of wit. His friend is also impressed with this work.

Gopal becomes more reassured everyday of his own perceptions and powers of irony. Almost every other night he fills up half a dozen pages of description and commentary. They then start on their journeys to editors—and return home.He gnashes his teeth in anger and despair. 'What has seized this brood of devilish editors?' he cries in anguish. 'They print all the time utter trash but won't look at anything I send.' Once or twice he is infuriated enough to write to the editors offensive letters, but the editors take no notice of these either.

Friends suggest, 'Why don't you show your writings to our professor? He may be able to give some useful hints as to why these don't get printed.' Gopal feels too shy to do it and so replies haughtily, 'What can the professor know about the literary world? If he is professor of literature his ideas have stopped with Chaucer and Shakespeare and Browning. How can he help us?' In spite of this contempt, next day at college he is seen hanging around the professor's room with a bundle of manuscripts in hand. As soon as the professor emerges from the room, Gopal clears his throat and says, 'I have a request to make, sir?' He gently introduces the subject, and offers to read his collected works to the good professor if he will permit it. But the good professor pleads that he would like to read the manuscripts at his leisure if the author would not mind leaving them with him. Gopal remains in great suspense for four days. And then the professor gives his verdict: 'Your English is good. You must go on writing. That is the secret of all literary success. You may also try to write a little more objectively and impersonally. I think. You know what I mean?' In addition to this, he has made, with a light pencil, a few markings on the manuscripts to show infinitives split, impossible grammar, and offences against usage. After this interview Gopal feels very happy. 'Even a big professor of English thinks my stuff good!' He is elated. His public has gone up from one to two. Editors and their rejections seem to be too trivial to bother about now. He writes more stories and sketches, dogs his professor's steps, solicits further advice and directions, till the professor definitely puts him off.

Very soon his desire to see himself in print returns and makes him miserable. Except for a momentary exhilaration at planning a new line of attack on editors and trying it, he knows no happiness. He makes a genuine effort to understand the moods and needs of editors. He reads handbooks on authorship and the craft of writing and such literature as 'How To Sell Your Manuscripts,' and copies down various bits of information from the *Writers' and Artists' Year Book*. He is also conversant with various tidbits about English writers. He knows that Kipling received a hundred guineas for a short story; he knows that another novelist could not earn enough from his novels to buy ink and paper, but persisted and became a best-seller with his sixth novel and now owns a big island with a fantastic mansion on it, a villa in the Riviera, and is paid three dollars a word in America. He knows among other things that Edgar Wallace could not get any publisher to advance five pounds on his *Four Just Men* which later sold over a million copies. Of course Gopal, the fine artist he is, would scorn to be compared with Edgar Wallace except on the commercial side.

Meanwhile life progresses, and his experiences become varied, and he forms strong, uncompromising opinions on all sorts of things. He is swayed by romantic impulse at times. The stupidities of certain social usages stir up his contempt; certain injustices in the mechanisms of social life make his blood boil. He knows all about socialism. He has completely understood the hypocrisy of priestcraft. He has had a peep over the abyss into which religion can sink. He values highly all human relationships; at the same time he is fully aware of the stresses and complexities which impair human conduct. His heart has bled at the tragic inevitability of compromises.

For a picture of everything odious and vile he always thinks of his father's younger brother, a prosperous landlord. This man holds, according to Gopal, that whatever exists is right; that women must slave for men; that widows must be burnt on funeral pyres; working classes must be suppressed and exploited; the lowest official in government service is a godly being and deserves worship; the man of wealth is the real image of God; the poor are the real trouble makers and must be interned in a camp outside the town. This uncle is a sort of dummy for all Gopal's bayonet practice. Gopal has made a figure of him in a long piece covering an entire exercise book entitled *Mahendra's Uncle*. Mahendra is Prince Charming in Gopal's world. He is everything that is delicate, sensible, and agreeable. His uncle who brought him up ever since he lost his parents is the villain of the piece. It would not need a very sleuth-like mind to see the resemblance between Mahendra's uncle and the author's. This uncle cheats his ward of his property, ill-treats him day and night, and imposes on him all his own vile standards. The climax is reached when Mahendra fails in an examination (an occasion to expose the falseness of all examinations), and the uncle insults and starves him, and thwarts, for the moment of course, his romance and defames his sweetheart before the whole town, but suddenly the whole situation brightens up when the uncle dies of cobra-bite or paralysis. A happy dream not marred by anything like the uncle's point of view.

I mention this story only to indicate the line of Gopal's development. His anger, contempt, admiration, vision and plan—everything is duly recorded in stories, essays, and skits; and his green trunk fills up with manuscripts and all the clothes have to be found another place.

He reads his pieces to his friend and one or two others who are likely to applaud but never question or criticize. For nothing irritates him so much as ill-informed criticism.

He has made a secret vow to himself: 'I will be an author even if I have to starve all my life.'

* * *

He has passed his BA and taken his degree. The two letters BA are like two wings and are expected to confer on him powers of flight. He is no longer looked on as a fledgling in the nest. People ask him what he proposes to do with himself. He replies, 'I am going to be a writer . . .' People laugh on hearing this. 'Ever heard of a person wanting to live by his pen! It is all right as a hobby. In my undergraduate days I too used to write a great deal, and Mark Hunter and Kellet complimented me on my command of the language . . .' says an elderly gentleman. 'Writing is no profession. You can't . . .' But Gopal has grand faith in himself and idealism. 'I can somehow make ten rupees a month with my writings. I can live quite comfortably on ten rupees a month, because I am not going to marry.' However, he is compelled to send out applications for appointments, to see influential persons, to hunt for testimonials, and so on. The combined forces of family and society drive him about in spite of his resolve. He rejects some very low-paid jobs, tries out one thing and another, and goes to Madras or Bombay or some other big city, carrying his green trunk with him. It is a grand Odyssey. He has every hope that his personality will overwhelm the editors.

With picked masterpieces in hand he sees editors in their own setting. Seeing them in the flesh gives him a great surprise: they seem to be all very mild and reasonable men. The masterpieces are left with them, but are always returned, with a word of cheer or encouragement thrown in. But to his question what they would like, their reply is vague and evasive. 'Study our paper and you will know. We are always glad to encourage new writers.'

After all Gopal meets an editor who gives him something to do because he knows the Professor of English and has regard for his opinions. It is a monthly journal with its office in a narrow street. The editor himself is a great disillusionment to our friend. He is an anaemic, feeble man, who seems to be weighed down by his spectacles. 'You had arts subjects for BA?'

'Yes, yes.'

'Will you review this book for me?' He pushes across an immense, ugly volume, containing papers read before some mighty conference to which delegates arrived from all over Asia. Gopal examines the book eagerly. 'Not more than two hundred words,' says the editor. 'You must return the book. I hope you know we don't pay for reviews.'

'Yes, yes, I know,' agrees Gopal at once, almost afraid that the other might snatch the volume back. He takes the volume home, feels very proud of the fact that he has been commissioned a work now; he has the feeling of an old writer when he declares to everyone he comes across, 'I have to review a book for . . .' He plods through the thousand and odd pages of the report conscientiously, and writes his ten or fifteen lines of review. He sees the editor and returns to him the book along with the review. He has a sense of great triumph. The editor looks through it and murmurs an acknowledgement.

Gopal goes back to his town with the green trunk. In due course the ten or fifteen lines of review appear in print, for which he waits and watches at the free reading-room table. He is elated to see himself in print after all. And I may now add that this is the end of his literary ambition and career. Within a year or two he is reduced to the state when he will be grateful for any work that will relieve him of the tedium of existence and bring him thirty or forty rupees.

After a great deal of recommendation and importuning he is taken in a local bank on thirty-five rupees a month. He sits over ledgers ten to six, and on special occasions such as half-yearly auditing of accounts, he does not leave his seat till after midnight. Very soon his marriage takes place, and in a couple of years he is completely submerged in family cares. These are the solid realities of existence now— ledgers and family. Looking back, literary life appears as a vapoury day-dream, and very soon the green trunk is forgotten and vanishes under a pile of other articles in the lumber room.

* * *

I have come across quite a number of persons who began like Gopal and ended like Gopal. This career, with its utter frustration, has always seemed to me very tragic. And this type of anti-climax seems to be peculiar to our country. With a view to finding out any general cause which may be responsible for it, I placed Gopal's career before a Man In the Street, a University Professor, and an Antiquarian, and asked each for his opinion.

The Man In the Street said: 'How can any man live by writing? I never knew people tried to sell what they wrote. One has to work for a living. Writing is no work! Besides, I suppose Gopal wrote some heavy, serious stuff. Personally I wouldn't care to look at anything which hasn't murder or love in it. These are the things which make a piece of writing interesting. After all, we read for relaxation . . . I hate all heavy and obscure stuff. All this apart, what is wrong with Gopal now? He has a job in a bank; thirty-five rupees is by no means a negligible salary. I think any one ought to be glad to be in his place . . .'

The University Professor said, 'Perhaps Gopal was third-rate. How could he ever have hoped to become a literary man?' 'But, sir,' I replied, 'it takes all sorts to make the world, and it takes all sorts to make the literary world too. Why shouldn't a third-rate man have a chance of trial and struggle?' The University Professor replied, 'Oh, it is this sort of attitude which causes decadence. I think the bank is the proper place for our young friend. The minor poet or the fourth-rate literary dabbler is a big nuisance, and it is good he is shut up in a bank.'

The Antiquarian said, 'Our educational system has a great responsibility in this matter. We have fallen between two stools. For generations the language of the soil has been called the 'Second Language,' and the training and application, consequently, has been second-rate. The 'First Language' does not easily strike root. This is a pititable condition and is more or less akin to loss of speech on a large scale. How can any first-rate literature come out of this?

'And secondly, our young friend is in a dream. When he thinks of literary life he thinks of only London literary life, and probably even counts his visionary rewards in guineas, while he is blissfully ignorant of our own literary traditions. In our country, the writer, or rather let me call him the 'man of books,' never viewed himself as a seller of a commodity and his readers as buyers. Literature as we understood it was not something that disappeared under an academic gown. Literature pervaded every aspect of life. The epics and *Puranas* had a bearing on everyday life and thought. Philosophy, metaphysics, religion, and every subject, reached the common man through the literary medium. Under the village banyan tree or in the temple hall the epics were read out, the minstrel recited his composition, or the pundit held his discourses, to an assembly. As long as the village copy of *Ramayana* or *Mahabharata* was there it was unnecessary for everyone to possess a copy; it was even unnecessary for everyone to learn to read, if he could listen to the readings under the banyan tree. There is a perfection in this utterly simplified relationship between a man of books and his public.

'That man had a grand world of his own, and he was not inclined to sigh for the goods of this world; he had also an austere disposition which made him demand few things of life. And the little he wanted was given him freely by his public, on every occasion possible.

'We have nearly lost all that. And we have not acquired in its place the immense technique of printing and publishing of the Western countries, where a writer becomes a cog in a vast commercial machinery. This halt between the two worlds inevitably produces tragic careers like Gopal's.'

The Average Man

by
R.K. Narayan

Since starting this journal I have been hearing a great deal about the average man. I am told that I must keep my eye on him if this journal is to prosper. People tell me, 'We have read this journal with great interest but we are afraid many of the articles appearing in it may be above the head of the average person. You must try to appeal to the average person.'

This, naturally, prompted me to look for this person. I did my best to pick him out in this crowded world. I kept my eyes wide open when I was in a bus or train or a gathering in the hope that I might catch a glimpse of him. I listened intently to other people's conversations in the hope that it might help.

This proved to be exhausting work. Very soon I realized that it was an impossible search.

* * *

The person who mentions 'average' invariably applies it to others. He always assumes that he himself is other than average—above, preferably, but never below.

From the context in which this reference is made I understand that the average man possesses the following virtues: Nature has endowed him with a robust constitution. He is very methodical in everything. He looks after his family correctly. He maintains a precise account of his income and expenses. He pays off his debts promptly. He sends his children to an ordinary, commonplace school. He is elated when they pass their examinations, irritated when they fail. He is industrious and honest and serves his masters faithfully. He is a good neighbour.

These are excellent qualities, no doubt, but they imply in a subtle way a set of parallel defects. He is hardworking because he is a born drudge. He looks after his family so well because he knows nothing else in life. He pays off his debts promptly because he has a sort of secret haughtiness which makes him say to himself, 'Why should I be under an obligation to anyone?' He is law-abiding because he is a prude. He keeps a strict account of his finances because he is disposed to be miserly. Even his health is so good because he is thick-headed and is free from the torments and exhaustions that beset a sensitive mind. Intellectually, he adopts the line of least resistance. The finer shades of literature and the arts are not for him. In books he can appreciate only gossip, sensation and buffoonery. In music he prefers the cheapest tunes, in cinema he demands the broadest melodrama. Politically, he is at the mercy of the loudest orator, and he can be beguiled with slogans.

It is supposed that he constitutes the bulk of the population and hence his goodwill is indispensable for the commercial prosperity of any undertaking.

After a laborious search I am almost convinced that this is an imaginary being— something like those mythical birds one reads about in any *Purana*. When people say, 'You must try and appeal to the average man,' they say in effect, 'You must work within the understanding of the average idiot; but don't make the mistake of thinking that it is myself.'

This notion of the 'average' person has caused a deliberate cheapening and lowering of standards in all creative work. I have known a publisher who at one time produced first-class literature, later on turning over rank rubbish by the ton on the plea that he was going to please the average person. I have heard a film director explaining away his costly rubbish with: 'After all, the man who really pays for the show is the average person.' I have known a director of a radio station spending months on a special programme and finally sending out on the air incoherent, inane noises, and answering all criticisms with, 'Our average listener will like this immensely. You will see how many letters we receive appreciating this programme.'

Anyone who has anything to do with the public conjures up a vision of an average man according to his own limitations, and on this basis sets out to give the public what it wants. The public, ever generous and indifferent, takes what is given with a feeling that it might be infinitely worse. This is understood by the other to mean that what he has given is slightly high-brow and next time he takes care to remedy this defect. And so goes on this race to get behind each other, between the public and the man who gives it its books, films, or music.

There may be an average person where economics or other social sciences are concerned, but in intangible matters like response to artistic or intellectual work, there can be no such thing as average. One must set about one's work, whether producing a film or a book or whatever it may be, with an eye on one's own standards and purposes rather than on the purse of an imaginary being called the average man. The average ought always to be reckoned at the end and not at the beginning since 'average' is not a cause but a result.

Letters

Letters

(The letters published below passed from a friend to another some years ago, and are now presented for their literary quality.

We are obliged to screen the identity of both the writer and the receiver of these letters.

I

My dear Friend,

I fear lest you be too busy to read at all. That you should reply is unnecessary. Better than all, come back to us soon. I find that when you are so long away I fear I may die before we meet again. True you have left me some kind friends here; but who has your voice? There are hearts as sincere and a hand-clasp as warm—but they are not yours. You always brought with you the music of many possibilities. We miss you each day more and more. This will not console you in your exile but it will, at least, let you know we do not quite forget you.

There is much I would like to speak to you about which I cannot well write. Doubtless you hear from other sources. You must have only indulgent friends. You have many. Most men would be perfectly satisfied to have but one friend and he a K—. In these days of acceleration and acquaintances it is getting as uncommon as apparently unfashionable to have friends: Now Mr K is not only a friend who finishes your sentences for you, but one who can speak for you. But there is no need for panegyrics. I prefer to offer affection.

Your brother-in-law has paid me one or two visits. He was here today. Sixteen students, Mr C.K.R., Mr B.K.S., his wife, two children and nephew, and Mr S—were here to-day at different times. The last-named gentleman was here from 9 am till 5 pm! I shall henceforth always refer to him when my wife cheekily asserts I 'bore' my visitors. If I do as she so positively asserts then Mr S—is an heroic man deserving not a medal but martyrdom. Truely he must know that

> *In this world of clouding cares,*
> *We rarely know, till wildered eyes*
> *See white wings lessening up the skies*
> *The angles with us unawares.*

To one like myself some people will always be welcome if they swing rich foam-wreaths on the waves of lavish life. And I love people to whom night brings the longer thoughts like stars. I have had dreams of glory in my nights of grief. Yet have I not also painted on the high plaster of my rooms—

Ye walls! sole witnesses of happy sighs,
Say not, blest walls, one word.
Remember, but keep safe from ears and eyes
All you have seen and heard.

My friend, shall I vex you with my varicoloured web of dreams? You are away in the wilderness and I am outside the world. So might we both say in one breath. I would rather be where you are. I wish in the cool of the quiet evening we could walk round the secluded policies of B—and then go up some tower of Protus to watch the lights bursting into blossom like so many budding stars upon the blue borders of heaven. There would I tell you how

In the cold star light on the barren beach,
Where to the stones the rent sea-tresses clave,
I heard the long hish of the backward wave
Down the steep shingle, and the hollow speech
Of murmurous cavern-lips, nor other breach
Of ancient silence. None was with me, save
Thoughts that were neither glad nor sweet nor brave,
But restless comrades each the foe of each.
And I beheld the waters in their might
Writhe as a dragon by some great spell curbed
And foiled; and one lone sail; and over me
The everlasting taciturnity;
The august, inhospitable, inhuman night,
Glittering magnificently unperturbed.

There might I tell you how I found that evermore the deepest words of God are yet the easiest to understand.

I fear I am exhausting your patience. So I shall slip my anchor and drift downstream to take some cargo that is waiting aboard— breakfast. Please convey to your wife my respects, and accept my most affectionate regards. Know I always wish you well, and will listen to you nineteen times out of twenty-five!

Also know that I seldom read long letters— I write them. I expect from you but ten lines in which you can tell us you are all as well as we hope and getting reconciled to your exile.

Au revoir! my dear friend.

II

My dear Friend,

I am depressed by much at present, particularly by a letter from on high and the news of a young lady for whom in common with my two brothers I entertained peculiar affection. She has left many of the roses in the garden of my soul grey and scentless. These things, however, have not kept me from thinking quietly of your mother and of you, who I love. Why do you always think in mortal terms? The dying deserve gratitude and envy. They do not desire our pity. You have a million years in which to

strive to become what your mother would have
you be where the soul sits free and all the noble
mothers await us to lead us into God's garden
where the eternal children foregather far from
the shady sadness of the world we must outgrow.
No words of mine, however, can console you for
the perished dreams of the past. You must
know, nevertheless, that you would grieve your
mother with your grief. Do not make her going
hence other than glad with the promise of
reunion. There is room for gratitude, joy, ecstasy,
calmness, none for sullen grief where a soul
waits the Invisible Ship which will return some
other day to take you to a shore where she will
await to welcome her dear children. Your loss is
great and keen, what is it to the gladness of her
great release? We lose each other but for the
holy rapture of recovery. But I have said enough.
I too—yea, even I can keep quiet and still,
content to hold the hand of my friend.

We are well, at least Madam is. I am not my
best self yet. Could you not come here for your
New Year's Day? My own birthday (and pay
day! alas, how it goes!) comes tomorrow, 1st
April. I know you wish me well. With all good
thoughts and most affectionate regards.

III

My dear Friend,

I learn of your sorrow with sadness and I send you such words as one sad heart may send to another wise enough to be willing to listen to it. I note with some surprise that you imagine yourself beyond the touch of philosophic acquiescence and the consolation of religion. What vanity is this? Is there not a peace in the calm azure of the unruffled deep, and some solace in the night lit with a thousand tender and sympathetic stars? It would pain me to die, if it were only at the idea that anyone I love would grieve too much for me. Why think of death as embarrassment; it is a blessing. If never before, then surely at the dark and dreary hour the generous affections stir about us. Then our enemies begin to cease hating us and our friends grow more loving. There is no thornless path leading out of life and few lying within it. Do you not think that age is but often death without the quietude of death? However yours is a sad vision at present and I regret I cannot be with you if only to hold your hand. I know how the salty bread of sorrow can be sweetened. The secret is to eat it in silence. There is such a thing, my friend, as ignoble grief. Yours must not be like that of the undisciplined and brooding angels. You know well, I think, that the deeper we descend into the vale of tears, the fewer illusions accompany us; we have little inclination and less time for laughter. Light things are easily detached from us, and we shake off the heavier as we can. Instead of levity we are liable to moroseness; for always near the grave there are more thorns than flowers, unless we plant them ourselves or our friends supply them. But you will be impatient of these almost cold-blooded words.

You have lived vainly if you do not already know that as everything has its use so life is here to teach us the contempt of death and death the contempt of life. We cannot conquer fate and necessity, yet we can yield to them in such a manner as to be greater than if we could.

I am afraid you are selfish in your grief. Why not think of the glad release where there is perfect peace, where the wicked cease from troubling and the weary are at rest. I am not much of a hand at writing condoling letters, but I will tell you plainly I am sad because you sorrow. Come to me and I will listen: you know not how well I can listen.

I will go—

I will go to my House of Dreams, will go where I may
hide
My bruised heart, which grief hath well-nigh
slain:
For there shall I find a shield for my wounded side
And a mask to hide my pain.

I will go to my house of dreams, will go where I may
slip
The stained garments of the world from me.
For Silence, there, with finger on her lip
And brooding eyes, hath made her sanctuary.

I will go to my House of Dreams, will go where I may
rest
My faint spirit wearied with all strife:
For Peace there will lay her hand upon my breast
And still the trembling pulses they call Life.

IV

My dear Friend,

Your envelope was addressed to me but the sheet enclosed to my wife. This, I suppose, is a form of joking peculiar to yourself! Next time please address the envelope to my wife and send therein an overdue letter to me. However we are glad you are alive and care at all to write when your town is so enervating as to render you incapable even of crossing your t's!

You have such a refined genius for ambiguity that neither of us knows to whose letters you really refer as providing you with infinite pleasure and having an ineffable charm. Perhaps this is as you meant it to be. Only why send me cryptograms? My friend, have you not heard the strange tale of a man who wouldn't write what he thought because people might think he was really trying to say something else? It is as sad as such tales usually are. For when his mother-in-law died he wrote how sorry he was and the people—being unable to decide whether he should be put into an asylum or to death for lying—gave him a new mother-in-law to console him for the loss of the one he bemoaned. All allegories have more or less intelligible meanings, I fancy, and I leave you to work out your salvation with this one.

Next week I will be somewhat busy. There are examinations, and I will have two sets of papers to correct. There are some beautiful days coming though after that. Then you should come to see me happy. Already some new books have come to hand but so far they are out of your piratical clutches. Just now I am taking things easy as I am not up to the mark. My throat is affected. So I dream with my eyes on the hills while the sun sweeps down on K's halls. One of my most recent dreams may interest you much, unless of course, you are getting sick of me and my dreams. What I call dreams are more real to me than you think. What shall it profit a man if he lose the whole world to gain his soul? I can guess but you will not thank me if I tell you. Anyway let us get to this most recent of visionary adventures.

I was thinking of Mount Joy and so my dream shaped itself. As softly as sin steals upon the slumbering soul, so came the dusk. Like some vagrant echo from the infinite, wavering and trembling like a timid bird, the dim vision of a soul's desire broke upon his consciousness like a wave far out at sea. The sky was peach purple and the moon was a thread-circle of light, like the marriage-ring of a woman who has long worked for her salty bread. One star, superb apart, in valorous isolation, flashed supercilious glances on the grovelling earth. From a lone house hidden among dark trees the sound of a strange sad music reached him on the heights. The glory of the dawn of night burst upon him and his thought was transfigured . . . Tonight the town he lived in was but a speck of sand on Illimitable Shores. It was like his own shadow, known but heeded not. Why had he come out on the hilltop in the cold and cheerless night? Rapture for the senses, but ecstasy for the soul, and ecstasy is born of silence . . .

* * *

. . . I will remind you of your friend Abdul Fazl's saying—Heresy to the heretic and religion to the orthodox, but the bloom of the rose petal to the perfume-seller!

Your gracious cousin was here recently. We find him a most charming man. He has only one of your bad habits and twenty good ones you don't care about!

Can you not tell us anything of your brother-in-law? Is he progressing or is he in prison?

Just as I write I see the silver-blue moonlit night before me and so I must leave you while I drink in the magic vintage of the wondrous night. My friend, can you not think it was on such a night that Anthony glided on the Nile to Cleopatra's imperishable feet; that Shah Jehan bade farewell to the Taj; or that Romeo set out to say farewell ere Juliet met Death, the coldest lover in the world; or that on such a night the great Buddha found Illumination, or Christ his disciples asleep when he asked them to watch...?

V

My dear Friend,

Your latest note proves you are a hedonist! To spend three whole days in 'Laughter and Babble' seems suspiciously like being deliberately vicious! Just now, however, I do not feel up to moralizing upon the grey vanity of things or of demoralizing you. My ways here are pleasant and so far all my paths are peace. Here I am content without being afraid of growing satiated. I feel calm without becoming callous. I sit watching the waning day and to welcome the moonrise. Sitting up in the verandah I note the opalescent sky against which Mr K's magnificient house stands like some hall of dreams imagined when music is no longer regret and memory becomes rapture . . . And my heart grows heavy; the vision of a happier day is clouded and if a bird sings, it sings strange songs upon a barren bough. The wonderful fire of sunset flares over the dark palace like some hectic dream . . . Strange dreams are these born beneath a pallid moon above a dark palace. From there the breeze blows hitherwards. There is only the loud music of silence across which trembles the ghostly sighs of some unseen tree touched into suffering by the passionate wind. Then the big star is blotted out by the wings of a vagrant bat and I think of the spoilt summer of a life when it has rained too long. Sometimes my thoughts range over the eternal pastures of the past and life for me is only a symbol and no longer a sensation. Or, it may be, it seems an echo of some music lost long ago when the argosy of my dreams beat about the high headlands of hope. How easy this facile pathos yet how real, do you know . . .?

Please rest assured I am succeeding very well in keeping my 'pledges.' I point-blank—but politely—refused to preside at some Association meeting last Sunday, and I do not think anyone will ask me again. My friend, I am just enough of a fool not to make consciously the same miserable mistake twice.

I am not going to say much more at present. When we meet and you give me a chance of speaking plainly without any comment I may say something about these and other things.

Otherwise please understand I am practising
Raja Yoga. It is so easy for me to make myself
understood apparently that I will thenceforth
have to placard my utterances even to you!
When I write plainly people imagine I am trying
to be practical: when I write practically people
mistake my purposes for the poetical. Is it
because I part my hair on the right side or
because I wear ties which would make a brass
monkey weep?

My time here is taken up with more
temptations than students. There is so much I
want to do, hope to do, mean to do, and am
trying to do. For example I have forty-six letters
to write this week! Only, mind you, I am not
growling or moaning and groaning about want
of time, peace, or anything else. I have troubles
and anxieties—these will pass, doubtless. The
great thing is to be glad that you and K—and a
few others—happen to be on the same planet I
am privileged to dwell upon! Is that not a
tremendous thought and a reason for much
gratitude? You remind me of the dawn—you
bring both gladness and disillusionment. Yet
you have much of the mountain tarn about you
too.

I trust your wife is managing to pick up
some strength and is feeling better, that all your
children are thriving and that your brother-in-
law is not causing you any anxiety. He is a
marvellous youth.

Goodnight. I leave you to the care of your fellow-angels.

VI

My dear Friend,

Your letter disturbed me today. You are the most morbid person in the world at the present moment. I am sorry you should have written as you have for you have no reason to complain about me. I do not doubt you have said nastier things to me than I have ever found it possible to say to you. However, if you are going to give all the kicks and take none I will send you a nice football with my initials neatly painted thereon by my own hand.

Why should you dwell so tragically on a grim *jeu d' esprit*? How can you honestly infer what you do?

> *The devil hath not in all his quivers choice,*
> *An arrow for the heart like a sweet voice.*

You evidently do not see very far or very deep. I am too perturbed in mind to observe your touchiness with that felicitious exactitude which will leave you the honey without the sting, the rose without the thorn, or the beautiful wine without its bitter dregs. Minor martyrdoms are cheap today. You have no passion for the pale moon-sickened solitude of my soul. You are a philosopher and I am a fool. What can you expect? I am not reviling you: I revere philosophers, especially when they are patient with fools.

You are wronging me every day when you say you are not as dear to me as you used to be. What right have you to think thus? Do you want a book of sonnets dedicated to you every six weeks? I never doubt your indulgent attachment, do I? You are the grave-digger of jokes. This is your only joke!

I am not sure if you are quite as good a listener as you ought to be or even so good a one as you imagine. But I am not going to 'bandy' words with you any more. You will have to give up your spasmodic-spontaneous criticisms. I am not so hopelessly idiotic as you seem satisfied to think. You must remember that we people don't willingly tolerate what you so philosophically accept as your portion in this world of sorrow. We work well when we get the chance and we will go on working steadily so long as you don't needlessly interfere with us. The pettiness of some of your men here is enough to make a flea grin . . .

I have been very busy removing and regret exceedingly that you never saw me in this house which it grieves me to leave.

So in the intervals of removing, I have been reading Keats to keep my head cool. You people who constantly reproach us for lacking wholeness and completeness of nature forget that because we are artists, this must necessarily be so. That very concentration of vision and intensity of purpose which is characteristic of the artistic temperament is in itself a mode of limitation. To those who are preoccupied with the beauty of life nothing else seems of any consequence. You ought to know that even in actual life egotism is not without its attractions.

I am very deeply grateful to Mr K for his great kindness in letting us go to his house. I will be perfectly happy there but I fear Madame will find it fearfully dull. Unfortunately, she has not my infinite capacity for doing without company. The place is sanative: the air, the light, the perfumes and the aspects of things concord in happy harmony. I may be idle but I never fear a fit of the 'blues'. Mirth, lyrical mirth, and a vivacious classical contentment are of the very essence of the art of my inner life.

I shall do well there and not write one letter to anyone unless my mother or brothers. These are the only people who never care how I write or speak.

My friend, I cannot help harking back to your irresponsible quibbling about my indifference. You do not seem to remember that the world has grown sick, having been so curiously tolerant of certain persons, separated by choice from the main-current of affairs and engaged in the contemplative life as thinkers, saints, or artists. You forget that there is another yet more finely-grained type of character, akin to those, yet distinct from them, for which the world at present apparently has neither room nor recognition. People forced by circumstance to this scintillating keenness of edge, have usually for their aim in life, my dear friend, a dutiful practice of giving to all things their eternal values. Their peculiar characteristic is a certain abiding wistfulness, anxious but without hope of real knowledge. Thus we seek rather to preserve a receptive attitude of mind than to put forward any definite propositions in the form of creeds, principles or philosophies. Mark the last! I suppose it is the penalty we must pay for distinction that we should be precisely diaphanous—a medium through which the eye might see all but not an object on which it can find repose. Alien to the strong dynamic forces of the world, in the great development of things, we shall be effective—not as Luther or Danton were effective—but contrariwise by our calm and titanic impotence—vicarious sacrifices to the outraged Furies who must be always be waiting round the shadowy corners of windy life.

I myself would never close my heart fast against the feelings of humanity. Nevertheless, I would calmly and critically consider by what conduct of life they may enter it with the least importunity or force. However I will sing to you

now as the mocking-bird to the rose, as the
moon to the lotus—

> *Lost to a world in which I crave no part,*
> *I sit alone and listen to my heart,*
> *Pleased with my little corner of the earth,*
> *Glad that I came—not sorry to depart.*
> *Why should it be that those who merit least*
> *Must always be the master of the feast*
> *The fool's purse fat, the wise man's ever lean*
> *and Beauty's self the harlot of the Beast?*
> *'Tis written clear within the Book of Fate*
> *The little always shall oppress the great,*
> *Who most deserve be slaves to those who least,*
> *And only fools and rascals go in state.*
> *To my house of dreams let the rumour run*
> *of the ringing reigns of old*
> *of horsemen riding in the sun*
> *Through worlds of windy gold.*

You must not get too big a dose all at once.
So I shall come to a close.

I am not going to beg of you to come or not.
You are still—I suppose—in possession of your
best faculties and I fancy you know your duty is
to come. I am sorry I am much too much upset
to be very good company but if you give Madame
your company she will be glad and possibly
grateful.

I am retiring from the world and I don't
think you will be very successful in getting more
out of me. Now I must die down like the angry
flare of the sunset sky into the dreary pallid
grey of the gloomy night of brooding.

VII

My dear Friend,

Your brief note has provoked a reply you as little deserve as expect.

I do not know what you call 'philosophic note'. However, you seem on the whole to have appreciated my few words with that *nil admirari grace* which so much suits your particular cast of countenance.

I am very pleased to be here in this retreat and can hardly know how to thank my dear friend for letting me come here. The beautiful noonday quiet here is something like the silence round the shores of sleep. The song of a solitary bird breaks rarely upon the ear and I hear the breeze breathing among the trees like an army sleeping in shadows.

The morning bursts out to bloom in the world like a region of fiery roses and the evening falls in one long wave of reluctant darkness faint and far. I watch the rooks trooping homeward like the stragglers of a decimated army without loot and careless of defeat. The flying foxes come out like so many lost souls seeking their remembered places amidst the haunts of the living.

And mine are those delightful tenuous thoughts of that eternal twilight land which lies between hope and remembrance. All the ecstasy of youth blends with that poignant melancholy which proves the pain of defeated memories. The stars come out like so many faint beacons— the distant flickering lamps of that splendid city which is set on the hills of hope and peopled with so many desires. The night is usually spoiled by the ceaseless noise of innumerable carts carrying back drunken braggarts to their villages.

When there is quiet I feel something of that serene spirit of peace which must possess the souls of the mighty.

Why should anyone feel dull here? Do not tell me it is all a matter of taste or temperament. For I am genial and sociable among the right people. I can enjoy the benedictions of the town too. It is a matter of that exquisite discipline which sustains the sanative soul. It is perhaps not quite true to say that solitude is the school for genius. I suppose the solitary souls in our big cities know well otherwise. Genius is never educated without strife. Is it not necessary to have chaos within in order to give birth to a Dancing Star?'

This beautiful and peaceful existence suits me perfectly. I have spoken to no one of the superior fools here for almost over a long month. Why should I? Must the monkey go to the crocodile to know what his own tail is like? It is so nice to be away from people you can never hope to find one single idea in common with, or whose poses and pretences long ceased to attract either one's pity or contempt. Suffer fools gladly—when you have to. That is as far as I will go.

There is an impression here among my fellow barbarians that I am a perfect young ogre: that I think no one here is good enough for my company: and that I keep Madame rigorously confined under my very nose lest they corrupt her or pollute her mind with their vulgarity and pettiness. It has afforded me much malicious satisfaction to know that this great fact has had a subtle and spontaneous generation in so many diverse minds equally endowed only in one respect—shameless dishonesty.

Who are these people? Because the land holds both cobra and crocodile must we make them meet? Where is the social, moral, or ethical code which insists that a man who is perfectly satisfied he is living quietly must go to hobnob with those of weak intellects and vicious souls? If you were a canary don't you think a donkey might well be surprised and distrustful when you requested to shake hands with it? If people want to know me let them come here.

VIII

My dear Friend,

Would you kindly explain yourself more clearly: you have recently made some very nasty remarks about me. I've just got hold of them. It is somewhat a pity that there is no doubt they are yours. The only doubtful factor is why on earth you did speak as you have done. I am not one who welcomes tittletattle: only as the world here is very narrow you might have recollected the certainty of those words reaching me. Perhaps it was because of such assured certitude that you have been so unkind.

Your reference to my humour and pleasure are in bad taste, so I need say no more.

I am shortly departing from here. Such books of mine as have 'found their way' to you might be left in Mr G's hands as I cannot come to your kingdom. All the same, thank you for your kind and strange invitation. It pleased me much to hear you are all well and I sincerely hope your house will be free of all illness for a long time now.

I have nothing much to say about myself that cannot be misunderstood unless that I am very sad about many things; in one instance over the death of a beautiful young lady friend of mine. However, there are infinitely sadder hearts than mine elsewhere, and it is, perhaps, part of that sorrowful discipline of the soul to remind myself that all the bounty of the spring cannot give reflowering to a plant that is wounded at the root.

IX

My dear Friend,

This is with us at all events—a season of Peace and Goodwill to all. But I need not have waited so long in order to have as benign an emotion. My reason is better. Your pride—have you not a beast within you called Pride—unless more villainous than I care to think it, could not unashamed refuse my greetings now. I have found you better than you have been.

The harm you have done me in bitter and ungenerous moments, in blind indiscretion, has left me only with a keener perception of your past kindness, with a fuller sense of pronounced value for your generous and exacting friendship and affection.

I am not quite as silly as you seem to be or as you seem to think me. I owe you much and have never been tardy to acknowledge it. And it gives me some pleasure to take advantage of the season and send you even this slight reminder of my gratitude and esteem. Whether you will accept it so I do not wait to ask. But if I have obtruded upon the inviolate sanctuary of your recollections too rudely, I trust you will pardon me if I have thrown a flower through a window I thought was my friend's.

I sincerely wish you well and trust you will have a successful year in and out of your house. I hope you will find good health and happiness always seated amongst you, invisible but always unwilling to depart.

Above all I would wish you to remember that every man has more loyal friends than he knows and, perhaps, you would not care to say of me that I have more friends than I deserve?

However, I must not vex you too much with this reminder of my presence. It will be enough to send you my affectionate greeting—to you all—and conclude by contending that if you are not my friend I am still grateful to be,

Your friend.

X

My dear Friend,

Your brief note has brought me much happiness. I am glad you took my red rose to your heart. But why should you 'not expect anything in the nature of compliments of the season' from me? That was not kind of you: for it shows you have little knowledge of me. Nay, worse, it implies a sad want of faith in yourself. The difference is—you choose to remember that I never forget.

I did not doubt you would send me kind

words and you have. You did not honour the good within me when you expected no remembrance from me and my letter has changed that.

Little do you know what secret influence a word, a glance, a casual tone may bring! Like the wind's breath on a silent harpstring a memory is thrilled into being, touching my inner sense like the light sweep of a bird's swift wing on a deep, still, and silent lake, wakening dreams that come from where I know not.

Did I not find your soft eyes through the dusk looking into mine and all the boundaries of time and place broke down; and far into a world beyond of buried hopes and dreams I beheld in a soft mirage of tender light your well-beloved face?

Let it be as you say: for our Past has but a sigh for epitaph.

Why—excuse such questioning—why should we pity those who weep? The pain that finds a ready outlet of salt and bitter tears is blessed and needs none of our sympathies. Look how the warm rain fits the shorn field for new yield of grain. It is only where brazen red skies beat down remorselessly upon unsheltered slopes that there is—drought. There, there is no relief. The anguish is long: it is a still, unuttered, silent, wordless grief. No sudden tempests or slow dripping tears, only an eternal aching. This is the sorrow wherewith hearts break and are broken. Think you not as I?

The world is wide, for those who love; but not for those who hate. How beautiful an experience to have found one of whom we can say.

> *Thy lips, as if endowed*
> *With potency divine.*
> *Changed with a word my life*
> *From water unto wine!*

Remember you are not the only flame-hearted lover and friend walking under the planet of Love! Your words have been as music to me. They have intoxicated my sad young heart. Is ecstasy but the apotheosis of anticipation: while I sit here I can see before me those memories with surge like legions of desperate dreams through the broken bastions of my sleep.

I suppose your mind, like most minds, must have felt the pathos of the story of the girl who leaves her village home to plunge into the deceptive excitement of life in a great city. She sends no word of her surroundings, but her father, month after month, year after year, sets the cottage door open each night, with the quiet words: 'Some day she will return.'

She returns at last, broken down in body and mind, the piteous wreck of her former self— brought back by love, the love which in her saddest degradation she had never forgotten, as it had never failed her—to find forgiveness which she had first despised and then despaired of, in her father's arms.

Of course the father's love had conquered; yet, touching as is the picture of the old man calmly waiting year after year, it was not his to put forth that greatest love, that went out to seek and to save the lost. I say she could not have sunk to the depths if she could be brought back by what was to her only a blessed memory. Such memories have often served only to repel.

My dear friend, the supreme love will not rely on a memory, however tender or compelling; it has other weapons. I tell you to follow the unfaithful friend or the wandering child into the abyss: to bear the ill-will of others, the odium of the sin, as if oneself the malefactor; to suffer the gibes and the contemptuous hatred even of the wrong-doer, until the old affection, wounded and half-dead from the blow of the unforgotten injury, begins to reawake from its stupor—this is the steep but royal path of complete reconciliation.

I know, too, and wonder if you do also, that in every age, human nature would have been infinitely the poorer had no tears been shed for the frequent sinning and the unmanly repentances of those whose own hearts had never known the pangs of honest self-condemnation. Suffering of this kind is the most potent means by which man influences man. It is not of course of the most conspicious. But the grass on the hill-sides grows green because of a thousand hidden streams which only rise to the

surface on the slopes far below. All those who
have exercised any empire or influence over the
inner loyalty and devotion of others have surely,
I fancy, wielded a sceptre wreathed with starry
tears of compassion.

But why should I give you all this—why? I
suppose you have inspired me to sermonize!

Yet, ere I pass to other things let me tell you
a little story. It is one of Gogol's, that golden-
hearted harlequin of Russian humour. I cannot
even remember what it is called; anyway I sh'all
give it a significant title, being influenced once
more by you when you write 'the chapter of
errors will close'—I will call my version.

Why We Should Keep Quiet.

The two Ivans were neighbours. They were
the greatest of friends. Never a day passed
without their seeing each other and their greatest
pleasure was to entertain each other at big
Gargantuan-like meals.

But one day they quarrelled—about a gun.
Ivan N—called Ivan P—a goose. After this they
would not see each other, and their relations
were broken off.

Hitherto they had sent every day to inquire
about each other's health, had conversed together
from their balconies, and had said charming
things to each other. On Sundays they had gone
to church arm in arm and outdone each other in
civilities. Now they never looked at each other.

At length the quarrel went so far that Ivan

P—lodged a complaint against Ivan N—saying that the latter had inflicted a deadly insult on his personal honour, firstly by calling him a goose, secondly by erecting a goose-shed opposite his porch and thirdly, by cherishing a design to burn his house down. Ivan N—lodged a similar petition against Ivan P—.

As bad luck would have it, Ivan P's brown pig ate Ivan N's petition and this, of course, made the quarrel worse.

At last a common friend tried to bring about a reconciliation, and asked the two enemies to dinner. After much coaxing they went. A large company had assembled. Both Ivans ate their meal without glancing at each other, and as soon as dinner was over made ready to depart.

They were surrounded immediately by friends who adjured them to make up again. Each said he was innocent of evil design and the quarrel was within an ace of being settled properly when, unfortunately, Ivan P—said to Ivan N— 'Permit me to observe in a friendly manner, that you took offence because I called you a goose.' As soon as the fatal word 'goose' was uttered, all reconciliation was out of the question and the quarrel lasted until the end of their lives. So endeth my tale!

> *Such is it that we can poetize thus:*
> *Some weep that they part*
> *And languish broken-hearted,*
> *And others—O, my heart!*
> *Because they never parted.*

Reviews

Reviews

Epigrams of Despair*

Francois Duc De La Rochefoucauld was born in 1613 and lived through the reigns of Louis XIII and Louis XIV as an aristocrat, politician, soldier, thinker and writer by turns. He yielded to an ardent desire, quite opposed to his simple nature, to take an active part in the politics of the times and only succeeded in getting involved in unedifying political intrigues from which he emerged scathed, embittered and chastened. His untimely devotion to Anne of Austria brought him up against the formidable Richelieu and landed him in the Bastille and finally led to prolonged banishment from his estates. The Queen, excessive zeal for whose cause brought

---

* *The Maxims* of La Rochefoucauld—translated into English by F.G. Stevens (Oxford University Press, World's Classic, Re 1.12.)

him to this plight, ignored him when she came
to power on the accession of Louis XIV. Piqued
at this, he joined the *Fronde* rebellion against
the Queen and Mazarin, again with more zeal
than wisdom, and received a wound that nearly
blinded him. Very soon thereafter, he passed
out of politics altogether, for which circumstance
the world of letters has to be thankful, for, he
now entered upon a life of literary activity
which gave the world, among other works, his
famous *Maxims*.

The *Maxims*, 568 in number, are brilliant
epigrams on subjects as varied as *amour propre*,
art and boredom, death and marriage, wealth
and old age. It seems both wearisome and
unnecessary to attempt to propound a philosophy
of La Rochefoucauld out of these fragments. It is
said that he was a 'psychological hedonist' as
revealed in the following maxim:

> We can love nothing except in relation to ourselves,
> and we do but indulge our taste and pleasure
> when we prefer our friends to ourselves.

His observations on human nature do no credit
to the persons with whom he came in contact. Of
human gratitude he says:

> Not only are men apt to forget kindnesses and
> injuries; they even come to hate their benefactors
> and are reconciled to those at whose hands they
> have suffered wrong. Perseverance in returning
> good and avenging evil seems almost intolerable
> bondage.

Friendship 'is merely partnership, mutual assistance for private ends, or a bartering of good offices; it is, in fact, a transaction from which selfishness always expects to reap some personal advantage.'

Particularly bitter are his references to women:

> Women may be found who have never had an intrigue; but she is rarely found who has had but one.

> When women give way to frailty, frailty is the least of their offences.

> The reason why women are not usually very susceptible to friendship is that they find it insipid after experience of love.

He is convinced that goodness deserves credit only in those who are strong enough to do evil and that in other cases it is usually laziness or want of character.

It is easy enough to understand all this bitterness in a man who saw life in the courts of Louis XIII and Louis XIV, and whose sacrifice and devotion led him only to the Bastille and banishment. When he took to writing, La Rochefoucauld had a disillusioned spirit and an impaired body.

La Rochefoucauld's reflections on death are also those of a cynic—a cynic who will not admit that there are men who can despise death. He dwells at great length on the unreality of the contempt of death. We may have various reasons for being weary of life, but we never have any for despising death. But in his *Portrait* of himself he declares that he has absolutely no fear of death, a statement which is said to have been justified by the way he met his own end.

This is an altogether fascinating book by a colourful personality, beautifully produced by Oxford University Press, which, those who don't mind iconoclasm of this vigorous kind, will much enjoy.

R.K.S.

*   *   *

Here are a few random selections:

> Our wisdom is the sport of fate, no less than our worldly goods.

> We rarely find people sensible unless they agree with us.

> An honest man may love with the zeal of a madman, but not with the levity of a fool.

> No quality is rarer than true benevolence; even those who imagine they possess it are generally merely of a weak or compliant nature.

> Young people on their first entry into society should appear shy or awestruck: a confident assured manner generally leads to impudence.

Speech That is Silver

'Persecution is a word so odious, and toleration a word so generally embraced that two opinions are not entertained on either; and yet, strange to tell, much difference has arisen upon the application of them.' The rafters of the House of Commons must have sensibly shook to these words uttered by Charles James Fox in 1792. And so it goes on, speech after speech on the constitution sifted by Mr Emden and elegantly published in the *World's Classics**. Do words merely conceal thought as the Gallic cynic would have it or do they mean more? Years later Benjamin Disraeli tells the world, 'I am not ashamed to say, however much as I disapprove

---

* *Speeches on the Constitution*, selected by C.S. Emden 2. Vols. (*World's Classics*, Oxford University Press. Re 1. 12.0 each.)

of the Charter, I sympathize with the Chartists. They form of a great body of my countrymen; nobody can doubt they labour under great grievances . . . little credit to this House if Parliament had been prorogued without any notice being taken of . . .' Political labels are mechanical contrivances of convenience. Life is an organic process and men who control life as part of the mechanism of socially organized power are more real than their party affiliations give them credit for. In every crisis men talk simply and comprehensively, and Mr Emden has provided us with an arsenal of freedom, a stimulus to clear thinking, an atmosphere which induces awe for man's blundering, infinitesimal efforts for realizing his humanity towards man.

In 1831 the Duke of Wellington thundered forth: 'If I am right in thinking this fierce democracy will be established in the House of Commons, does any man believe that harmony can continue between the King and his Government and the House of Commons . . .' While George Grote a few years later said, 'Let the elector vote . . . he will have no perils to defy and no temptations to resist.' The speeches give us hope in man's ultimate good sense. It is believed by some of the modern speculators that the mutation in evolution has now to take place on the psychical plane, consciousness has to break its individual 'fetters and liberalize itself; the body has gained universal dimensions thanks to the technique of science and is now as uncouthly and stupidly heavy as the ancient dinosaur; any fresh advance, forward thrust in evolution has to be on the mental plane. If that is so, the time for it has surely come, my masters. And what other country has revealed in talk, in discussion, in persuasion, the universal implication of the business of a 'polis' better than 'this sceptered isle . . . this England'. Hearken to General Smuts (April 1917): 'In all common concern there should be effective arrangements for continuous consultation . . . that there is an exchange of ideas and that the system, whilst preserving freedom and equality in its parts, will work with a strong sense of unity at the centre.'

And so it goes on, whether it is the People and their rights, the Sovereign and his relation with the different parts of the Constitution, or the rights of the supreme legislative will of the People. Discussion is a solvent of cynicism even as cynicism is the groundwork of dictatorship. Through meeting and getting together, even if it be at the point of a sword (wielded by nature or human nature in its brutalized form) men see the flickerings of sanity against the dark background of eternity. It is time we imported decencies, urbanities, courtesies, of ordinary life, or a professional ethic into the realm of politics where even honour among thieves has been non-existent. And unto this last and if possible greater purpose Mr Emden has urged us with the choir of heaven and furniture of political England a blessing on his venture.

K.R.P.

Teeming Million Speaks*

'I only wanted you to realize that India is a country of which you and I may well be proud. Whether India can be equally proud of you and me is, I am afraid, altogether another matter!' says Mr Minoo Masani in his book *Our India*. In 166 pages of fascinating narration, vivid arithmetic and illustrations, Mr Masani achieves his purpose and also tells us what we are to do in that 'altogether another matter'.

The variety and wealth of India, which have been there all along, are brought home to us with a new force, and in this, the hundred graphic illustrations help a great deal. India

---

* *Our India* by Minoo Masani (Oxford University Press. Price Rs 2.12.)

has a vast population, one out of every five persons in the world being an Indian. India has a vast area, being as big as Europe minus Russia. Its climate varies widely: 125 degrees in the shade in some parts and below freezing point at others; rainfall can be anywhere between 460 inches and 3 inches per year. There is abundant sunshine, vast areas of fertile land, many mountains and rivers and rich forests. But there is also poverty and premature death; the men in charge of India's largest industry, agriculture, are ignorant; their cattle starved for fodder; their lands in fragments and badly tilled. The raiyat is fool enough to burn all the cowdung as fuel and starve the land, and the monsoon is always up to its old tricks. Out of this quagmire the Indian is to be salvaged by means of co-operative farming, canals, afforestation, modern machinery and better, if fewer, cattle, which last is to be achieved by our eating the extra cattle that find nothing to eat. This done we are to proceed to the planned industrialization of India and lest the owners of capital should begin to grow rich and oppress the poor, it is proposed that key industries should be nationalized and the smaller industries owned by individuals and co-operative groups.

The author's means of achieving certain ends, in themselves very worthy ones (e.g. dealing with cattle), may not find general acceptance, but in a land of many opinions and perpetual arguments, nothing that awaits general acceptance will ever get done.

The book is, very appropriately, entirely Indian, being made of Orissa bamboo and Jaipur cotton. The printing and finish are excellent.

R.K.S.

Surfeit in Poetry*

The decline of Swinburne's reputation as a poet is largely due to the feeling of satiety which he unfortunately produces in a reader. The beauty of his poetry lies in its use of sound. This use of sound, with all its implied suggestions and symbolisms, was clearly conscious and deliberate on the part of Swinburne. But a poet must have a rich and varied experience of life to draw upon. Swinburne, as it has been aptly pointed out by Harold Nicolson, responded to very few 'stimuli' in life. All this had been absorbed in his personality before he left Oxford, and the poetical output of his later years was merely a continual ringing on the same diffused experiences—the sea, the wind and some revolutionary feelings.

---

* *Swinburne: Selections*. World's Classics, Oxford University Press. Re 1.12.0.

This monotonous repetition of the same theme practically bores the reader.

So Swineburne can be enjoyed only in sections; the Oxford University Press have done the reading public an inestimable service in bringing out a representative collection of his poems. The poems in this collection bring out the specific qualities of Swinburne—the cadence of his verse and the mastery he has over the lyric.

Laurence Binyon observes that in his earlier poems, 'We are exhilarated by . . . Swinburne as by the lovely motions of a dancer, but hardly moved. The language is, so to speak, a non-conductor, it is there for its own sake. But with . . . Shelley there are vibrations that come from a world of felt experience and intimately modulate the rhythm. The language is communicative . . .' He quotes two parallel passages from Shelley and Swinburne to prove this. But at his best Swinburne escapes from this bondage of sounds and words. In some rare moments he can be simple—even as simple as our Upanishads or the Bible.

> *I the grain and the furrow*
> *The plough-cloven clod*
> *And the ploughshare drawn thorough,*
> *The germ and the sod,*
> *The deed and the doer, the seed and the sower,*
> *The dust which is God.*

But such moods are rare in Swinburne. Often he loves to clothe his thoughts in a rich foliage of words and metaphors. Sometimes, of course, the thoughts are completely smothered under the weight of these poetic paraphernalia:

> *Shall she live*
> *A flower bud of the flower bed, or sweet fruit*
> *For kisses and the honey making mouth*
> *And play the shield for strong men and the spear?*

But the tendency to condemn Swinburne *in toto* must be resisted. 'It may be,' says Laurence Binyon in his introduction, 'that with reaction against harsh matter and deflated rhythms there will come a revived enjoyment of Swinburne's clear and confident singing voice. But, because his sensibilities were so different from those of other men and so extreme in themselves, he is likely to remain to a certain degree isolated and remote. We must take him for what he is; we expect from him no broad and deep humanity, no tender intimacies of perception; but he has done things that no other English poet has done, and in his own special sphere he is supreme.'

K.V.

The Poetry of Valmiki

by
Masti Venkatesa Iyengar

'The *Ramayana* first went to the people as a poem. Religion thereafter took hold of it. To release it from this hold and treat it again as a poem is to do it service,' are the words we find in the introductory chapter of this book entitled *The Poetry of Valmiki*. Mr Masti Venkatesa Iyengar must be considered to have saved the poetry of Valmiki by claiming poetry as poetry.

The *Ramayana* alone among the epics has enabled the Indian mind for long to visualize a hero, who was a man by birth, but who by his conduct and deed became God. There may be persons who strictly interpret the *Ramayana* as

(Copies can be had of the Author, 43-44, Gavipur Extension, Basavangudi Post, Bangalore City. Price Rs. 3.12.0)

the story of God who became man. We need hardly dwell upon such controversies for the very reason that the author of this volume has saved us the trouble. For, as a matter of fact, it is proposed in this book by the author to study the *Ramayana* as mainly a poem. This does not necessarily indicate an irreligious attitude. For Mr Venkatesa Iyengar knows as much of our religion as any other Hindu, and what is more, he knows that poetry and religion are not really different compartments. 'By claiming poetry as poetry, we claim to make righteousness permanent.'

We may feel it strange that the arrangement of the sixteen chapters in this volume should be such as to place the *Salutation to the Poet* in the last chapter. Normally, one would expect this chapter at the beginning and not towards the end. Perhaps we can give no plausible reason for it except that Mr Masti Venkatesa Iyengar's inborn restraint and genuine love of Indian culture has reserved the fitting homage to the last, after preparing us for it. We cannot but remember long after closing the book, the significance of the following sentences which occur in the concluding paragraphs of the book: 'Indian youth, educated in the modern way, may value Shakespeare and Milton, and Voltaire and Tolstoy as high as ever it likes, but it ought not to neglect Valmiki . . . 'Will you rather your Indian Empire or your Shakespeare,' asked

Carlyle, imagining a situation, and said that he would rather give up the Indian Empire than Shakespeare. 'Indians have no Empire to lose: they have only Valmiki and his like.' We can only add to this kind of writing words which occur again in this chapter and which again remind us of the deeper significance contained in them, namely, 'Valmiki indeed is one of the sources of India's hope for the future. His large heart, open mind, deep vision and rich utterance came from this population. Something like them is no doubt still there in its constitution. It is finding expression in various lives at various times and is giving us continued proof of its persistence.'

The book is written in a delightfully simple language and for that very reason claims our admiration. No doubt the subject is an old, old one. And scholars there may be who will not readily accept the suggestions made here and there with regard to interpolations in the text of the *Ramayana*. But his true inwardness will, we are sure, make the readers feel amply recompensed for their attempt at understanding the heart of a supreme poet whom India honoured in the past and still claims to honour as the *Adi Kavi*.

There is a certain amount of *naivete* in the narration of the story of the *Ramayana* by Mr Venkatesa Iyengar; he gives us the same impression even in his titles to the chapters, such 'The Story of Six Books', 'The Household of Dasaratha', 'The Story and Four Characters', 'More of the Story' etc. There is no attempt in him to attract; it is all, from beginning to end, simplicity at its best. But even the most cultivated of modern minds can find an inexhaustible store of artistic impressions and critical literary appreciation, skilful narration and poetic insight in these chapters. The later chapters, containing general observations about Valmiki's 'Powers of Description', 'Civilization and Culture', 'Some Questions', 'The Valuation of Valmiki', will prove an abiding source of help to those who have not drunk of the original, but who cannot repress the emotions that are generated by a sense of pride that they also belong to a country which has produced Valmiki.

It is often said as a point of criticism against the later day Sanskrit poets in general, that they lack originality, for the primary reason, that many of the themes they chose for drama, lyric and didactic poetry, were taken from the three great epics. If only the critic could closely follow the minds of our ancients and the way in which the ideals of life and civilization have been held up in their works, he would easily come to the conclusion that nowhere else could be found so much of matter for moral elevation. He will also readily agree that of the three epics, the *Ramayana*, the *Mahabharata* and the *Bhagavatha*, the first alone makes the greatest appeal to his artistic emotions as a single unified poem. The qualities for which man has striven in the past and will ever continue to strive in order to reclaim himself from barbarism, have been envisaged in the personality of Rama with a rare vision by this great poet of India. If today civilization has lost much of its original significance, which India had realized in the conception of 'Dharma', the story of Sri Ramachandra as depicted by Valmiki will point out to the erring Western nations the high watermark of civilization that India alone has known.

'C'

Modern Verse*

There is a certain class of scholars fed mostly upon a diet of the old classics, to whom modern poetry is anathema. To speak before them of the merits of modern poetry is to blow the bugle for battle. The present volume of selections would without doubt go far in allying their fears that poetry has dried up since the good old days of Morris and Rossetti and Swinburne. The editor sets before us a fare which, though sparing, is yet appetizing. It is not easy to apply an infallible touchstone to discover true poetry, but if poetry is taken to be the revelation of life by an inspired artist, a large portion of the present volume would easily pass the test.

Naturally difficult as it is to give an exact date to when the new tendencies in poetry made

---

* *Modern Verse* 1900-40. Ed. Phyllis M. Jones. World's Classics, Oxford University Press. Price Re. 1.12.0

themselves manifest, the period after 1910 may be roughly taken to herald the new age. Nonetheless there were a few not inconsiderable poets before this time who came as the vanguard. Before the publication of the *Anthology of Georgian Poetry* in 1911, Symons and Dowson had begun shocking their generation with their aesthetic audacities and sensational sensualism. Bridges had already written much and his poems show not merely metrical felicity but that pellucid purity generally associated with the old Caroline poets. Oscar Wilde had written his famous *Ballad of Reading Gaol*, the last sincere gasp of a lurid existence. Kipling with his faith in the white man's destiny had begun stirring the public with his rollicking *Barrack Room Ballads*. Yeats, as Humbert Wolfe points out, had produced the first draft of the constitution of the Free State in his *Lake Isle of Innisfree*.

The Spirit of the New Age may be summed up in the words of A.C. Ward who gives the modern poet's manifesto thus: 'I recreate in my poetry the world I perceive; not the world seen by Shakespeare, or Milton or Keats or any other. I strive in my poetry to communicate my own perceptions; not to make you see what I see but to recreate for you the experience I have in my unique perception of the universe and in the unique universe I create about me from the material of my own sensations.' Thus the gallant Rupert Brooke sings with an almost Keatsian fervour of the simple and thrilling joys of the old and lovely earth. W.H. Davies praises the luxury of an idleness as of the gods while the accents of Walter de La Mare have the *naivete* of the old ballads with the fairy magic of William Blake. Harold Monro and D.H. Lawrence have the gift of turning out finished ivory-works of poetry faultless in word and picture. Flecker is glamorous as the East of which he sings while Masefield brings out the old-time romances of far-off spots. In sheer lilt and romp of words Chesterton's *Lepanto* is hard to beat, while the elegant artistry of W.J. Turner is indisputable.

Soon in the wake of these poets came the Great War and resulted in a fresh outburst of inspired music. In the first glow of feeling, men felt as though they were born again. The times were stirring, youth was thought to be eternal and it was a great thing to die for a noble cause. Henceforth the rifle and the knapsack became the symbol of glory. Thomas Hardy's *Men Who March Away* sings the exaltation of a soldier as he marches to war. A.E. Housman gives the perfect pen-picture of a soldier exchanging love for war in the delicate tripping lines *The Deserter*.

But shortly comes the disillusionment when war is seen as it really is—the curse of the earth that snatches away the good and the strong. The initial glamour past, men become aware of the grinding unhappiness of the common soldier on the battlefield. Collective patriotism gives place to a surging tenderness for individual victims of the war. The poignancy of a sudden and unknown death amidst the war is brought out in the grim lines of Wilfrid Gibson's *Breakfast*. The tragedy of many a soldier whom death claims in sleep is well pictured in the terse and intense lines of Wilfrid Owen's *Asleep*. While what war can do in souring the human spirit is seen in the bitter lines of Siegfried Sassoon's *Base Details*. Robert Nichols paints the fine picture of a soldier who recollects his home in the stern reality of a battlefield.

A volume of selections may be expected to do a double service. It must first entertain and delight the reader with what it provides: secondly, it should stimulate effort to study the subject on a wider compass. This fine anthology of modern poems does them both—and does them well.

A.C. Seetharama Rao

Revelations

(Studies in Biography.
Oxford University Press. price 3 sh. 6 d. net.)

Ten important contemporary writers like G.D.H.
Cole, Naomi Mitchison, G.K.C., Capt. Liddell
Hart and Stephen Gwynn, write about men and
women who have contributed to English history
and letters. The subject of the essays cannot
interest an Indian to the same extent as they
can interest an Englishman. To the latter, they
have an immediacy of interest as Shivaji has to
us—even though centuries place themselves
between the character and the reader. Chesterton
takes pains to prove that the romance around
the name of Mary Queen of Scots is only a
legend, and that the ill-fated woman had great
political wisdom. *Goldsmith* (by Stephen Gwynn)
is more interesting because it is more
biographical, though Mr Gwynn takes care to
point out Goldsmith's achievement in many

branches of English letters. Mr Edward Marjoribank's account of Gladstone is a little too controversial. Mr Cole contributes an interesting account of the versatile Morris, and says, though not in so many words, that William Morris was a first-rate man who produced second-rate things. Morris today is remembered more as a socialist than as a poet and his was the aesthetic approach to socialism. (It is a pity that this approach is rarely heard of these days.) This world around us should be made a beautiful place and that can only happen when work is not a synonym for drudgery, but a pleasurable activity. Work should be a means of self-expression and all the things around the worker should be beautiful. This led Morris inevitably to socialism. These are days of scientific Marxian socialism, and anyone who took his argument from Morris would perhaps be considered old-fashioned. But, personally, I like the approach, and India especially must needs be taught it, as we are threatened with a crop of Vinoba Bhaves, puritans crying down every kind of beauty and joy in life.

The most attractive biography in this book is certainly that of Dr Elizabeth Garett Anderson, the first woman doctor in England. We are taken back to those days when women were thought unfit for any profession except the one that nature obviously intended them for.

Capt. Liddell Hart's account of Foch is

challenging and perhaps promises a clue to the French debacle in the present war. Foch put the doctrines of Mrs Eddy Baker and Emile Coue to test on the battlefield and the result—thousands upon thousands of English and French lives were needlessly sacrificed. Foch realized, in the end, after paying a heavy price, that even the most determined of will has to be backed up by mechanization. It is a pity that the French did not profit from the lesson.

M.N.S.

National Socialism and Christianity

N. Micklem
(Oxford Pamphlets)

The Church must ever clash with the State, preaching as it does loyalty to something that claims to be above the State. The refusal of the Church in Germany, both Protestant and Catholic, to acknowledge Hitler as the Messiah of the New World, and to adapt its tenets to the Nazi way of life is the cause of the conflict. Hitler for his part finds Christianity promoting disloyalty to the State, as 'effeminate'. ('Universal love is a blow at the soul of Europe') and so has started his own pagan religion. Another fact that emerges in this booklet is that a number of German Christians are Germans first and Christians next, and these have been used to strike at Christianity in Germany. No weapon has been too mean for the Nazis in their efforts to wipe out this particular enemy.

M.N.S.

The Nazi Conception of Law

J. Walter Jones
(Oxford Pamphlets)

One will be surprised to learn from this pamphlet that there are law-courts in Germany! They seem to be quite unnecessary when there is the Gestapo: as a matter of fact they are. Nazi law is founded on the very theories that the Nazi state is founded on: the leadership principle, the racial theory, the concept of *lebensraum* and a hundred other crotchets of the Fuehrer. In fact, a German writer stated: 'Nazi law is nothing less or more than what the Fuehrer decrees.' 'All law,' says the Nazi, 'must be frankly political.' Law must adjust itself to the changing political surroundings. But Nazi law is only for the pure unadulterated German race. The 'impure' races have no right to claim the protection of law. And

this is how crime is treated in Nazi Germany.
No wonder they say law is not a matter of logic,
nor of reason. It is a new way of life. And all
this just serves to make the Nazi system more
hateful and contemptible than ever before.

M.E.B.

Propaganda in International Politics

E.H. Carr

(Oxford Pamphlets)

No political movement can be successful unless there is the consent of the people behind it. If any political act is to be a success the people must be satisfied as to its merits. Hence the necessity of the art of persuasion in the sphere of opinion. In that, the principle of laissez-faire is decidedly suicidal. Thought must be nationalized. This is no less necessary in peace-time than in war-time. 'Psychological war,' says a modern writer, 'must accompany economic war and military war'.

Curiously enough, the word is derived from De Propaganda Fide, that institution of the Catholic Church, the sole office of which was the propagation of the gospel and the suppression of any antagonistic creed. Propaganda, therefore, implies not merely dissemination but censorship as well. It is a very good instrument of publicity. If the League of Nations did not succeed it was because no proper propaganda was done on its behalf.

Hitler says, 'By clever persistent propaganda even heaven can be represented to a people as hell and the most wretched life as paradise.' It may be true if all people are gullible. But, for propaganda to be effective, the people to whom it is addressed must be enlightened. And one of the curses of education is that it teaches man to think too much. However eloquently, therefore, the propagandist may try to represent black as white, people won't readily accept it. Thus propaganda will defeat its own purpose. A people cannot be hoodwinked for all time. There is sure to be a realization of this great crime of imposing on the intellectual faculties of man, and that may lead to a revolt. So Mr Carr here rightly suggests that propaganda, if it is to achieve its end, must always 'approximate to the truth' as far as possible, 'it must appeal to some universally or generally recognized values.'

M.E.B.

Books Received

Oxford Pamphlets on World Affairs
(Price 3 d. each)

Russian Foreign Policy by Barbara Ward, *The Fourteen Points And the Treaty of Versailles* by G.M. Gathorne-Hardy, *Economic Self-Sufficiency* by A.G.B. Fisher, *The Arabs* by H.A.R. Gibb, *'Race' in Europe* by Julian Huxley, *The Treaty of Brest-Litovsk and Germany's Eastern Policy* by John W. Wheeler-Bennett, *The Refugee Question* by John Hope Simpson, *Britain's Blockade* by R.W.B. Clarke, *The Danube Basin* by C.A. Mcartney, *How Britain's Resources are Mobilized* by Max Nicholson, *The Gestapo* by O.C. Giles, *Mein Kampf* by R.C.K. Ensor, *The Blockade 1914-1919* by W. Arnold-Forester, *The Baltic* by J. Hampden Jackson, *Turkey, Greece and the Eastern Mediterranean* by G.F. Hudson, *The Sinews of War* by Geoffrey Crowther, *Labour under Nazi Rule* by William A. Robson, *Colonies and Raw Materials* by H.D. Henderson, *Blockade and the Civilian Population* by Sir William Beveridge, *Czechoslovakia* by R. Birley, *The Life and Growth of the British Empire* by J.A. Williamson, *War and Treaties* by Arnold D.

Menair, *Encirclement* by J.L. Brierly, *India* by L.F. Rushbrook Williams, *Who Hitler Is* by R.C.K. Ensor, *Was Germany Defeated in 1918?* by Cyril Falls, *The Naval Role in Modern Warfare* by Admiral Sir Herbert Richmond, *Living Space and Population Problems* by R.R. Kuczynski

FROM MACMILLAN

Great Men of India by G.D. Khanna, M.A., B.T. (12 As.) *Scenes from Islamic History* by Syed Mehdi Imam, M.A. (Oxon) (Re 1.4), *Great Saints of India* by G.D. Khanna, M.A., B.T. (12 As.) *Scenes from Indian Mythology* by Syed Mehdi Imam, M.A. (Oxon)

From J.V. Doddaveerappa (Bangalore); Bhaktha Siriyala Setty (in Kannada)

The Secret Splendour

by
K.D. Sethna
(Review by Paul Brunton, PH.D.)

K.D. Sethna is a rising star in the Indian literary firmament who is well worth watching. With this slim volume of nearly one hundred pages he makes his debut to the larger world but I have been familiar with his work since the time, several years ago, when he showed me at Pondicherry the yet unprinted manuscripts which were then being privately circulated among a few lovers of poetry.

Whether he writes of Nature's nocturnal beauty or of man's tender love for woman, a single immortal theme runs right through his finely-spun phrases: the quiet quest of

(Published by the author: 47, Warden Road, Bombay.)

communion with the Overself, the profound aspiration to reach the Ineffable. An exalted spiritual awareness is manifest throughout the stanzas which are here strung together. In the words of his final poem.

> *If each delightful cadence*
> *Mark not a flight to Thee,*
> *My fancy's airiest radiance*
> *Profanes its own mute core of mystery!*

One is impressed by the picturesque words and Pre-Raphaelite metaphors in which the poet sets off his thought or limns his vision. He is a poet for the artists. But music is lacking and melody is absent. Sethna does not sing; he gazes, enthralled, at gorgeous visions and writes down what he sees.

The poem which I preferred most—not be it frankly confessed because it was necessarily the best but because I adore eventides and make their vigil my religion—was the one called *Sun-Spell*. This is how it opens:

> *In cloud-suspense the faint breeze died;*
> *A deep glow spread on every side;*
> *The firmamental hush came down,*
> *A mirrored soul of aureate brown*
> *Subduing each form-shade to one*
> *Pervasive ecstasy of sun.*

His pages are not simple; they are as complex as his highly-cultured mind. They are luxuriously ornate and bejewelled with costly gems. They carry an air of aristocratic distinction.

> *I had not bargained to behold*
> *A rhythm of cerulean gold*
> *Nor with an aching mouth impress*
> *Calm firmamental nakedness!*

Here is a powerful verse from *Himalaya*:

> *The tides of gold and silver sweep the sky*
> *But bring no tremor to my countenance;*
> *How shall sun-rise or moon-ebb lure, when I*
> *Have gripped the External in a rock of trance?*

And then this swift descent to *Modern Love.*

> *Amid the whining of the saxophone*
> *And the swift whisper of the dancing feet—*
> *Amid the music's strangle-throated moan*
> *And hundred swinging bodies' colour-heat,*
> *She lures me with far world-triumphant lips*
> *As though in one brief thrill of ecstasy*
> *A wandering voice of epic destiny*
> *Haunted the rhythmic swaying of her hips.*

Sethna's work will be welcomed by all those who appreciate poetry of high quality, clad in fine print and paper to match. This volume will assure his status in the front rank of contemporary Indian writers. I hope its reception will encourage him to produce another soon.

The Poetry of W.B. Yeats*

by
Louis Macniece

I very much doubt whether there is such a thing as new and old in poetry; only, as it were, a travelling illumination passing from one area to another of a continuous and indivisible surface, bringing out what a particular age wants to see. In other words, each age deserves its poetry. When we take this as our stand-point, there is no call for any particular age to characterize another as brilliant, shoddy, or cheaply sentimental. In the same way, the latter Victorian swing-away from the tradition of complacency and its formulation of the doctrine

---

* (Published by the Oxford University Press. Price 8sh 6d.)

of 'Art for Art's Sake' is justified. Its chief prophets from Rossetti and Arnold to Prater and Oscar Wilde were really sick of

> . . . this strange disease of modern life,
> With this sick hurry, its divided aims,'
> Its head o'ertaxed, its palsied heart . . .

and withdrawing from

> . . . this iron time
> Of doubts, disputes, distractions, fears.

became other-wordly, or in the words of O'Shaughnessy,

> We are the music-makers,
> And we are the dreamers of dreams;
> Wandering by lone sea-breakers,
> And sitting by desolate streams;
> World-losers and world forsakers,
> On whom the pale moon gleams . . .

These were the poets of the Nineties. Their doctrine was from Prater and their models from the French Symbolists. Yeats was no exception; he was enormously influenced by Prater but he was shrewd enough to stop with paying lip-service to Pater's aesthetic atomism for he was always trying to think of the world as a system, of life as a pattern, unlike Pater to whom the moods were more important and more vital.

Yeats then, 'learned to think in the midst of the last phase of Pre-Raphaelitism.' But he had to discard the facile theories of the Nineties for he could not correlate this pale aesthetic outlook with the 'sickness' of everyday life, especially in Ireland. But, to the end, he had a nostalgia for what he himself called, 'a new religion, almost an infallible church of poetic tradition, of a fardel of stories, and of personages, and of emotions . . .' He travelled very far, though, from the doctrine of Escapism and became a realist to whom

> Money is good and a girl might be better.
> But good strong blows are delights to the mind.

From the 'gardens near the pale of Proserpine' Yeats had arrived in the Civil-War-torn Ireland as the champion of Fascism and as a verse-maker for O'Duffy. He had evolved himself from an identification with the Japanese poets and lay-brothers dreaming in some medieval monastery into an old bellows full of angry wind; from an 'escapist' he had become a particularly brutal sort of 'realist'.

And here he is on common ground with Louis Macneice, one of the quartette singing of the Post-War Disillusion, but it is only superficially so. As Macneice himself admits, 'People who know my own expressed views on poetry might consider me unqualified for writing on Yeats, whose expressed views are so often the opposite of mine.' But he has been very fair, and what is rarer, he has been very objective and has tried to present Yeats not as Macneice sees him, but as Yeats himself. Still, Macneice cannot forsake his own canons, and he does judge Yeats according to them; but not to the exclusion of recognizing that 'Our ways are different; but that does not mean that I cannot let you live'. And he has succeeded in proving that 'Yeats, granted his limitations, was a rich and complex poet, who often succeeded by breaking his own rules and who turned his own liabilities into assets.' Which is rare praise indeed from a poet, critic and iconoclast who has been suckled into a life of cynical despair by the Post-War weariness.

K.J. Mahadevan

A Woman of India*

(Life of Saroj Nalini Dutt)

by
G.S. Dutt, I.C.S.

The conception that the Hindu woman has all the joys and duties of her life within the four walls of the home is a thing of the past. She has marched a long way with the times. She no longer sits absorbed in family duties, but 'is a woman who works for the weal of the home and community alike'. Such is the ideal of the present age and no life could be a more striking illustration of that ideal than that of Saroj Nalini, the heroine of this little volume.

The wife of an I.C.S. Officer, Saroj Nalini, like many of the members of that class, might

* Oxford University Press. Price: Rs 2/-

well have lived a life of ease and luxury had she liked. But she would not do it. She preferred a very different sort of life. She saw the woman of her country as backward, illiterate and living in purdah, which was a serious block to progress. Saroj Nalini wanted to lift them from this sad condition and make them live freer, happier and more useful lives. She rightly judged that women themselves should be stirred up and made to join in an united effort for their own emancipation. For, the force of such a combined effort alone, she found, could effect the solution of the social needs of the country. With this object in view, she established Mahila Samitis in a great many places in Bengal. How these organizations sprang and grew up through the extraordinary zeal and devotion of a single lady must make a most interesting study to all who have intelligence and the spirit of social service in their hearts.

Mr G.S. Dutt, the author of this book, gives an engaging account of the personal traits and character of his wife; how without being old-fashioned and orthodox she yet loved to retain those customs which she thought were good for the women of her country. She did not despise, he tells us, to wear conch-shell bangles and to put a touch of vermilion at the parting of her hair every morning after the fashion of Hindu women. To please him, he says, she spoke in

English, affected the Western method of dressing her hair and even took lessons in ballroom dancing all for a period, but gradually she made him realize that none of these things were natural and becoming to the people of her country. These are small things, no doubt; one can see nevertheless that these require a character and a definite strength of mind.

It is perhaps rather an ideal picture that we find here, painted by the glowing love of a husband. But the life of Saroj Nalini certainly illustrates how a woman can blend in herself all that is best in both the past and the present age.

The fact that the poet Tagore and C.F. Andrews held her in such high esteem as can be seen from the foreword, is the greatest tribute that can be paid to a life, brief but beautiful in its sweetness and simplicity and high-minded service to others.

K. Savitri

USA

by
D.W. Brogan

This short and shrewd book gives the best reading within its compass. Only a century ago, America was a young, prolific, mainly British and overwhelmingly Protestant nation and today it is rapidly moving towards middle-aged stability with very great Catholic, Jewish and Greek Orthodox minorities. The size of the country and the variety of the racial origins of the people, if considered, the degree of unity attained, is marvellous. A hefty bone for the contemplative Indians to chew.

Catholicism is strong in America, if numbers are considered, but it is Protestant in a far deeper sense than a mere statistical statement can convey. It emphasizes preaching rather than

Oxford University Press. Price: 2 sh 6d.

sacrament, the Bible rather than Church organization. America has no specific religion; all its important cults are based on Christianity. The American people wish all Churches well, so long as they do not thrust in the name of morals—standards of conduct too completely unlike those practised by the average citizen. The average American is suspicious alike of a Politician who takes too lightly or a Preacher who takes too seriously the role of organized religion in American life.

The size of the country accounts for the absence of national papers in America. No paper has a general circulation outside its own immediate region. The American Press has far less effect on public opinion and is far less an indication of public opinion than tradition asserts.

Though the gentleness of the American law of Libel can encourage certain recklessness in an editor he is often timid and is generally influenced by 'the great advertising moguls'. As the film industry hurt the stage, so the radio has taken the power out of the press and is directly shaping public opinion by 'fireside chats'. The people like to hear their leaders rather than read about them.

In this book, Mr Brogan has not attempted either temporarily to divert or permanently convert the reader. He is just instructive.

R.K. Pattabhi